Deal Finance

Tim Luscombe

Tim Luscombe

ISBN: 1499646461
ISBN-13: 9781499646467

DEDICATION

For Zita

CONTENTS

Tim Luscombe

ACKNOWLEDGMENTS

My thanks all the many friends and colleagues who have given freely of their time and knowledge.

INTRODUCTION

Over the many years I have been advising business owners, I have often observed how challenging the whole area of corporate transactions can be. The finance team in the smaller business is very unlikely to have had any real world experience in this area, and can only advise on the theory.

Many advisers in the corporate finance marketplace are only involved for a short time – it's another skill set to add to their CV. The experienced advisors in the larger firms often take the initial meeting, but then hand off the actual work to the junior team, helping them gain the experience they need. That's great for them, but not so good for your business or for you.

You may only get one go at this – so it needs to be right.

For smaller businesses advice is in very short supply. There are a number of business "Estate Agents" who provide listings of business for sale – either in print or on-line, or both – but do not provide advice for the business owner thinking of buying or selling..

The accountants who are the most trusted advisors for many business owners may have a partner who specialises in corporate finance, but many do not. It's another service they may offer, but the in depth experience is in short supply.

The general understanding of transactions is not helped by the news coverage, where the press are only interested in disaster stories and the transactions that go wrong.

The mass market entertainment programs that masquerade as business programs portray the investors as all knowing and quite terrifying. That's not really true – of course they have extensive experience and probably don't suffer fools gladly, but outside the TV studio they are not the demons they pretend to be. Most business investors know that they cannot succeed without the team, and need the teams to be motivated, focussed and on their side. It's not a truly adversarial process.

It is a complex area, filled with jargon and people who love to use buzzwords and acronyms. This book will cut through much of the clutter and help you do the best possible deal.

1 RESPONDING TO AN APPROACH

If you run a successful business, sooner or later the chances are that someone will approach you with an offer to buy your business.

When that happens, an awful lot will be going through your mind. Here are a few thoughts:

- You were not thinking about selling, but this might be the opportunity to secure your retirement and your family's future.
- You don't know if anyone else would be interested in buying your business and you have heard how difficult it is to find a buyer
- Is the buyer serious, or just out to get hold of confidential information?
- Will my staff find out?
- Will my customers / suppliers / bank find out?
- How much will they pay
- What's my business worth
- Where can I get help?

It is most likely that any initial approach is just that – an initial approach, with very little detail. It will raise more questions than it answers!

It's not an unreasonable parallel to think of this as if it were a romantic relationship. Step 1, you've been asked "Would you like to go for a drink?"

You may know the company making the approach, but there's always more to discover.

Respond by asking for a non-disclosure agreement (NDA) to protect your confidential information. They are usually mutual – in other words you also agree not to use the information you gather about them except to consider this opportunity. Look out for clauses that grant them exclusivity – in other words that you will not enter into discussions with anyone else – as it is far too soon to commit to that.

Find out about the person asking you out. You'd ask around & do your research first.

Research the company making the approach. Look at their website, use Companies House or a credit checking service to gain an idea of their financial health. Look for news stories where they are mentioned, especially if there are any stories about other businesses they have acquired.

If everyone tells you they are OK, you'd probably go on the date – but it would only be for a drink in a public place!

Meet the principal of the party making the approach. This should be on neutral territory, ideally where it is unlikely anyone who knows you and your business will observe you – so if you are in a small town, consider meeting in the nearest large city.

Your purpose is to get to know them, and to see if you like them and can get on with them. Ask them about their business, the vision, why they have made the approach. They will want to gather information from you, but at this stage you don't tell them anything that is not already in the public domain – for example on your website on in your accounts.

It is perfectly OK to say "I'd rather not disclose that at this stage" during this conversation, but it's a very poor idea to embellish the facts or attempt to mislead the potential buyer.

The acquisition process is very detailed so any attempt to distort the facts s will come out later – which would be very embarrassing. There's a fine line between "telling the truth – well" and misleading, so if in doubt, say nothing.

You will create a good impression if you talk about how you started, your vision for the business and how proud you are of what you and your team have achieved….but don't give the impression that you are bored, and it is time to retire or do something else!

Once you've had that first meeting, you will have formed an opinion of the potential buyers. You need to discover the answers to two key questions:

Do you like them?

If you don't like them or at least feel able to tolerate them it is very unlikely that the approach will come to fruition. For the buyer to get to the point of making a formal offer they are going to need to spend considerable time with you and you will have to share information with them.

In your background research, and probably explicitly addressed in your conversation will be the question of financial resources.

Can they afford to buy you?

One rule of thumb is size; typically the sweet spot for a company making an acquisition is a multiple of between 3 and 10 times the target. If the target is bigger than 1/3 of the buyer, that's probably too much of a mouthful not only in terms of value, but also to be able to successfully integrate the businesses. If it is less than 10% of the acquiring company it's not going to make a real difference to them.

The big exception here is where the purpose of the acquisition is to acquire intellectual property – for example in technology or pharmaceutical – rather than the operational business.

You've just had a first date, so you are some way from jumping into bed!

It is far too early to talk about the value of the deal. You will want to know how much they will be prepared to offer, but they won't be able to make a judgement until much later in the process, and if they do suggest a number at this point it will either be in such a wide range of values – recently a client was approached with an "offer" where the lower value was £2m and the upper value was £3m – or it will just be disappointing.

Get Help.

If you think they are serious, and you are not prepared to dismiss the opportunity out of hand, the next step is to appoint a corporate finance advisor.

You want the best value for your business, and that's not going to happen without some care and expertise.

Ask your accountant or trusted advisor to recommend a corporate finance advisor. It is often the case that your accountant will tell you they can do this for you, but you really want a specialist.

Accountants are not generally good salespeople, and if they don't do this on a regular basis they will not be good judges of the value of a business.

This will be one of the most important steps you take.

Ideally, the advisor will have dealt with companies that are similar to your own in size and sector or can demonstrate an understanding of your sector. The advisor must be someone you trust.

They will help you
- evaluate the acquirer and properly understand their reasons for considering acquiring your business.
- judge the worth of your business to the acquirer and also to a wider market of acquirers.
- position the strengths and benefits of your business in the mind of the acquirer to your best advantage.
- agree the agenda for each meeting with the acquirer, coach you on what to say and how to make your pitch.
- review and check all the historic and forecast financial and non-financial information you will provide to the acquirer.
- by chairing every meeting between you and the acquirer.

For the advisor to really help you, you need to decide on several things – the advisor will help you through the pros and cons of each, but these are your decisions.

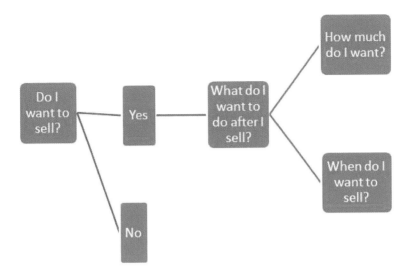

Do I want to sell?

The first and most important question is "do I want to sell?" If the answer to that is yes, or even maybe, the next question is

What do I want to do after I sell?

It is very likely that the acquirer wants you to carry on for a period after the deal is done. How long are you prepared to stay, and in what role? For many business owners, this is one of the hardest things to come to terms with. You've been your own boss, with little accountability to others, for many years, and now you have someone providing direction.

Usually, that role post acquisition is for a limited period of time.

It is possible that you will stay with the combined organisation in a new role, but that is only rarely the case. You'll need to decide what you want to do when your involvement with the company comes to an end.

How much do I want / need?

That's important because if you are no longer earning and you want to spend time improving your golf swing, you'll need one level of financial resources.

If you want to travel the world and live like a king (or queen) you'll need more money.

If you want to start another business (you'll be prevented from starting in the same industry for a while) you may need money to fund the start-up.

There may be assets in the business that you will want or need to transfer out, prior to the sale, and your corporate finance advisor can help with determining if this is the case for you. Often this will be the transfer of property from the business to your pension fund, which will then lease the property to the business. The acquirers are unlikely to want to fund the acquisition of the property or be bound to the premises for any significant period.

It is worthwhile consulting your IFA at this stage so that you can properly plan your financial future and determine how much you really need from the sale of the business. The IFA will be able to consider your pension provision and advise you.

When you have completed this review and you understand what you need from the business, your corporate finance advisor can compare that to the value they believe the business carries.

Smaller shortfalls in value may be recovered through deferred or extended payment options dependent upon the performance of the combined business, so you will need to consider how confident you are about the quantum of future profits.

When do I want to sell?

If there is a larger shortfall, there probably will be opportunities for you to increase the value of the business prior to sale. That takes time so you will part company with this potential acquirer. You will need to commit to a lengthy period, perhaps 3 years, to significantly change the fundamental value of the business.

It is also possible that there is a life event – a significant birthday, your partner retiring or something similar – and it makes sense to coincide your exit from the business with that event. Bear in mind that the sale process will take the best part of a year, and that you may (probably will) be required to be available to the new owner after the deal completes.

This buyer or look for others?

If you've decided that you do want to sell, and together with your corporate finance advisor you believe the business that approached you is a good strategic fit, able to fund the purchase at a level you would find satisfactory and serious about completing the deal you can enter into further discussion.

If there are doubts about the acquirer, then you should consider going to the wider market and looking for other potential buyers.

You will get the best value from a buyer who has a strategic reason to acquire your business. A good corporate finance advisor will help you identify the types of buyers and how to approach them.

The next steps

If you are moving forward with this buyer, the next stage is to get together your financial information.

- You will want to have your accountant involved and prepare detailed accounts with supporting schedules (ideally an audit file) so that the buyer can not only see the results, but also trace them through to the source.
- You will need to provide tax calculations.
- You will need detailed budgets for the next year, profit and loss and cash flow forecasts for the next three years.
- You'll also need to prepare non-financial information. Prepare or update a business plan for a 3-5 year period, profiles of the management team and a clear assessment of their strengths.
- All of this information can be used by your corporate finance advisor to put together an information memorandum, should you decide to go to the wider market.

Ready to pitch?

With all this information available, you'll be able to position your business in the best possible light for the acquirer, illustrating how they would benefit from combining the two businesses. Your corporate finance advisor will help you develop this "pitch".

Ready for Due Diligence?

The acquirer together with their lawyers and financial advisors will want to examine in great detail everything about the business, and it is a good idea to start preparing to answer their questions and provide the information.

Due Diligence is never easy! It feels as though you have to provide every piece of paper from the beginning of time.

Here's a generic check list of the areas you'll need to think about:

Statutory records
- Memorandum and Articles of Association, Incorporation Certificate, and any changes since incorporation.
- Summary of official company policies and procedures.
- List of subsidiaries, including details of purpose, ownership details, key personnel, and date of set-up or acquisition.
- List of partnerships and joint ventures, including summary of purpose, profit sharing arrangements, and start date.
- List of shareholders and their respective holdings, including holders of warrants, options or similar.
- Ledger of shares in issue including evidence of share certificates issued.
- Documents relating to any recapitalisation, reorganisation or restructuring since incorporation.
- Minutes of all general meetings, board meetings, and copies of the resolutions passed.

Finance
- Full-year and interim financial accounts, including audit reports if applicable.
- Quarterly management accounts.
- Financial forecasts, including financial model if applicable and cash flow forecast.
- Summary of all credit facilities or arrangements, including instruments of debt, leases and guarantees including copies of any significant correspondence with creditors.
- Copies of any significant correspondence with professional financial advisors.
- Any significant reports or recommendations from external consultants.
- Copies of all tax returns filed on behalf of the company and any correspondence between the company and tax authority.
- Fixed asset register, and schedule of current assets and intangibles.
- Details of all previous and prospective acquisitions and disposals.

Staff & HR
- Details and CVs of directors and officers, and summary of all other employees.
- Organization chart showing lines of reporting and management.
- Employee remuneration details and plans, including employee share option scheme, and benefits available.
- Details of any employee or directors loans, or similar arrangements.
- Details of appraisal and personal development procedures and plans.
- Details of relevant trade unions.
- Details of recruitment agency arrangements.
- Details of any previous TUPEs.

Legal
- Details of all previous, current and possible litigation, court orders, legal disputes, tribunals, or arbitration, including outcomes or terms of settlement.
- Details of any previous, current and possible litigation, legal disputes, tribunals, or arbitration, on the part of directors or officers, for example bankruptcy proceedings, or malpractice.
- Contracts of employment and director service agreements.
- Any notices of breach of contract either sent or received.
- Copies of any significant correspondence with external legal counsel.
- Any orders, demands or significant correspondence from regulatory bodies, law enforcement agencies, or government authorities.
- Details of any previous, ongoing or expected investigations.
- Any material government permits or licenses, exemptions, or terminations of such.
- All statutory filings other than financial accounts.
- All significant agreements relating to current and expected revenues, and key customers.
- Master Service agreements, contractor agreements, consulting agreements, retainers, or other significant service agreements or commitments with any external parties.
- License agreements, royalty agreements, or similar.
- Agreements relating to all acquisitions, disposals, mergers or any other change in the ownership or capital structure of the company, any subsidiary, or significant assets or securities.
- Agreements relating to the issuing of shares, share ownership, and any derivatives such as share options, including related rights such

as pre-emption.
- Copies of all deeds.
- Copies of all significant credit agreements and leases.
- Non-disclosure agreements or confidentiality agreements.
- Any extraordinary agreements outside of the ordinary course of business.
- Any formal amendments or terminations of existing agreements.

Intellectual Property
- List of registered, pending or applied-for patents, and other official registrations of intellectual property, in all territories.
- List of any registered or applied-for trademarks and other official registrations of trade mark or name.
- Details of previous, outstanding or expected claims of infringement or misappropriation of patents, copyrights, trademarks, or other intellectual property rights.
- Register of all significant intellectual property owned and in development.

Miscellaneous
- Long term strategic plan or business plan.
- Significant external communications with shareholders or other stakeholders, including annual reports.
- Summary of any significant marketing communication, publications or material.
- External analyst ratings or reports.
- Details of all significant insurance policies.

There's a lot to get ready, and much of it is highly confidential, but if you do agree an acceptable offer, you will have to provide this information very quickly – within a few weeks at most – so it is a good idea to prepare.

You will need a legal advisor once you have an acceptable offer, and selecting the right advisor is once again very important. The lawyer you use for the day to day operation of the business is probably not the advisor you want to use for this transaction.

Ask for recommendations from your corporate finance advisor and your accountant, but make sure whoever you choose as a legal advisor is experienced in corporate transactions. They will probably be more expensive on a daily or hourly basis, but they will be much quicker at getting to the heart of the matter.

Conclusion

When you are approached to sell your business, the timing may or may not be right for you, but it is flattering and exciting that someone wants to buy your business (and give you lots of money.)

It is vitally important that you consider your options with a rational approach and taking good advice.

You will find it very difficult to make any decisions without at least having exploratory meetings to learn about each other. Until you do that you just don't know enough, but you are not committed until the final paperwork is completed.

Whilst you are finding out about the approach, you still have a business to run and a team who will be worried and doubtful about the future if they hear of these discussions. You may pride yourself that you are open and transparent, but sharing the fact that you are in discussion with a potential acquirer can create nothing but FUD, Fear, Uncertainty and Doubt.

If you decide that the timing isn't right, or for some other reason this is not the deal you want to do, consider your options for improving the value of your business in the next chapter.

Tim Luscombe

2 MAXIMISING BUSINESS VALUE.

Steven Covey's Second Habit of highly effective people:

Start with the end in mind.

Most businesses don't start with an end in mind. Many of them start almost by accident and those that survive and grow are often too busy in the day to day battle for survival to consider an exit.

If you do nothing the chances are that your business will not continue without you.

Received wisdom is that 75% of businesses do not sell, and that only 8% sell for a premium. If you do nothing, the chances are you will not be able to sell your business.

Your business may represent your life's work.

It may represent the future for your children.

Its success is certainly down to your investment, not just in financial terms but also your emotional investment. You've invested time, sacrificing personal and family life over the years. All those "investment" factors have been integral to developing and growing your company – and creating the value it has today.

Ideally, from the day you began your business, you should have planned how and when you would exit and what would be the exit route. If you are raising money, especially equity finance, you'll need to have an exit route for your equity funders.

How do you exit?

There are many ways to exit your business, but the key to choosing the right route for you is to identify what you want from the sale.

For many owner managers, the continued employment of the team who have helped grow the business and the continued success of the business carry a significant value.

These are broad categories and are by no means mutually exclusive.

One way of ensuring the future of the team – or at least giving them control of their destiny – is a Management Buy-Out (MBO). There is a chapter on MBO's in the book, but here is an overview from the sellers' perspective.

MBO deals are often quicker than a sale to a third party as the buyers already know the business, but there are some disadvantages to consider:

• An MBO team is unlikely to be able to match the value offered by a trade buyer as they will not achieve any savings by combining businesses.

- The MBO will probably have to take on debt (or even equity) financing from a bank or other financial institution. This is a significant commitment for the management team and will almost certainly require that they put personal assets at risk.
- The vendor will have to accept payment over a longer period of time, so that it
- is not a clean break from the business which is now run by someone else – even though they are still using your money!
- Consider the fall-back position. How will the relationships between you (as the owner) and your management team (as prospective buyers) work if a mooted deal fails to materialise. Will the business be damaged by a management team with poor motivation?
- Is your management team up to the job? MBO deals have a very strong track record of success and are consequently relatively easy to finance, but often in the smaller business the vendor has been the entrepreneurial leader. That leadership is a vital part of the team which may not be a characteristic of the remaining members

"Why is this a potentially attractive route for Vendors? Depending on their involvement, the employees should already possess considerable knowledge about the business they are acquiring – staff, customers, suppliers, operations etc. This should facilitate a smoother transaction and subsequent handover than alternate sales. This also gives the Vendor the comfort that their business, which even at exit they are likely to retain an emotional attachment with, is being led by competent management. The likelihood is this presents the best basis for business "continuing as normal"." (Borzomato, 2014)

Some of the problems inherent in an MBO deal can be reduced or even eliminated through a Buy-In / Management Buy-Out (BIMBO) type of deal.

In these deals the existing management team is joined by one or more external individuals. Typically, these are experienced senior managers who are seeking the leadership role that was not available to them in their previous employment.

These problems still remain:

- A BIMBO team is unlikely to be able to match the value offered by a trade buyer as they will not achieve any savings by combining businesses.

- The vendor will have to accept payment over a longer period of time, so that it is not a clean break from the business which is now run by someone else – even though they are still using your money!
- The buy-in members of the team are strangers – not only to you, the vendor, but also to the other members of the team. BIMBO deals have a good track record of success, but often members of the team fall by the wayside as the new leadership becomes established.
- BIMBO's are often backed by financial institutions (Venture Capital) who set demanding performance targets and are quick to act if these are not met.

One of the more obvious routes to exit is a Trade Sale which is a sale of your business to another business. This is often a competitor.

You will get better value for a sale to a competitor than to an MBO or a BIMBO, but

- Your business, as you have created it, will be changed dramatically.
- The management team and staff may not have future employment.
- Approaching a competitor is a high risk strategy

Similar challenges apply to selling to a supplier, but there may also be issues with continuity of supply. If you sell to one of your suppliers, will they want or be able to buy from your other suppliers? In the same way, selling to a customer has challenges – they may not be able or willing to sell to your other customers.

A trade sale to a strategic acquirer is the route from which you will obtain the maximum value. The buyer will be a business that can gain from the addition of your business not just by eliminating costs (as with a competitor) but by leveraging what you have through the combination with what they have. A simple example might be the opportunity to cross-sell their products and services to your customer base.

A sale to a Diversifier is a sale to another business not already operating in your marketplace. This can be advantageous but again, the diversifier may not be able to match the offer from a trade buyer as they may not achieve synergistic savings.

A sale to a Financial Buyer is a sale to a hands-off investor who does not wish to take any part in the day to day management of the business. This buyer may appoint their own business leader, or they might combine with the existing management team in an MBO.

Many business owners also consider "going public" or offering the shares of the business to the investing community through a stock market.

There are two major disadvantages to this in that it is not an exit for the key management. If you are involved in the leadership of the business, you will have to stay involved and committed to the business for some considerable time.

A secondary disadvantage is that the cost of a flotation or initial public offering is relatively very expensive.

Whichever route you are considering, allow plenty of time to get your business in shape for sale. Typically a buyer will look closely at organizational and financial changes made in the three to five years prior to sale and will want to be confident that any such changes are well and truly embedded in the structure and culture of the business. Any doubts they may have about those changes will increase their perceived risk and reduce the value they are prepared to place on the business.

Preparation for sale.

Some of the actions to prepare for sale will be obvious and can easily be compared to selling your house or car. You tidy up, clean the house & polish the paintwork, you may redecorate, gather all the paperwork together and so forth, but selling your business is different. You will probably only do this once and by definition you are a novice at it!

When you prepare the car or the house, you have a good idea what the buyer is looking for and what they will find attractive. Equally, you know where the weaker points of your house or car are.

Any acquirer is most likely to buy your business for the future profits it will bring. Their guide to what these future profits may be is the historic performance of the business under your ownership, coupled with their knowledge of changes they would make. It is worth noting that the acquirer will value the business on its performance under your ownership, not its potential performance with their resources and investment.

You work in your business and are probably (not always) "too close to the wood to see the trees".

An external assessment of the business will cover many of the following areas

Your Role.

Are you the key to the business? Does it stop if you are not around? If you say "yes" to both of those, then perhaps you haven't got a business, you've got a job.

You can have a role in business development, and in managing the business, but the more you are a "doer" the harder the business will be to sell.

I was invited to review a client's business and found that he was central to everything that happened. No one else (in a team of more than 20) was allowed to make decisions beyond the straight-forward day to day operations. The team did not have job descriptions, let alone targets and objectives. My client had tried (unsuccessfully) to sell the business before I met him, and in the process had had a heart attack.

We put in place a structure for the team, with objectives and responsibilities. The owner is working a 5 day week (down from 7) and is now developing new business opportunities.

Track Record.

Do you have a solid track record of increasing sales, margins and profits? A premium price will only be achieved for businesses that can answer with a resounding yes.

My client has been approached to sell his business, but his track record is patchy. The uneven profitability over the last few years results in a valuation that he finds disappointing and the offer from the prospective buyer is unlikely to be accepted.

The root cause is very large projects – one project they are pitching for now will span two financial years and will be worth the equivalent of a year's turnover. If we don't accept this offer, we will develop a secondary stream of smaller projects to "fill in the gaps" if a project is delayed or deferred, as has happened in the past.

Customers.

Does your business have a good spread of customers? If one customer represents more than 20% of your business, that's a potential problem that will put buyers off.

A manufacturing business I worked with a few years ago had an order / production scheduling board with customer names / products. When we dug into this, about 80% of his business was with the one company that had bought all his customers, so that they were no under single ownership.

How many active customers do you have? Too many can be as bad as too few.

If you only have a handful of customers, the risk is that one can leave and you lose a lot of business. If you have a large number of customers, you must invest heavily in customer service and operations. Measure profitability by customer and make sure you leave behind the customers who cost you money.

A client had several thousand customers, and a customer service team who were harassed and struggling with the workload. When we analysed the business by customer, we found that the most profitable business came from the top 20% of customers. We introduced minimum order values and increased distribution charges. The number of customers declined by about 15% but profitability increased.

Where do you get your customers? What's the marketing program that captures prospects, what is the sales program that converts them from prospects to customers?

Many small businesses get their business by word of mouth or by reputation, but that's a difficult thing for an acquirer to rely upon.

A client has been in his industry (the building trade) for more than 20 years and has always won business through his technical excellence and from referrals. We have helped him break into new markets with a direct mail marketing program.

Are all your customers the same type, or do you have many different types?

A client of mine is a florist, who serves a broad range of different customer types from corporate events to weddings and from hotels to retail premises.

Who holds the relationship with the customer? We've all heard of the key salesman who when he left took all the clients with them. How many contact points are there between your company and your customers?

One division of our business was successful with a pitch for new business at a high profile city based client. Our sales team leader built a strong relationship, but when he moved on from us we lost the client to his new business. We made it a policy that the sales team worked in pairs, and that the technical support team made direct contact with the clients' technical team.

Markets Served.

What are the characteristics of the market you serve? If you are in a limited, or niche market, that is much less attractive than a market with wider horizons. Is it possible to sell your products and services to new markets, and if so why haven't you done so?

How strong is the competition in the market? If it is very competitive, and deals are won on price, your margins will suffer and so will your valuation. If you have a USP and can command the highest price that is much more attractive.

Is your market growing, and at what rate? Selling into a declining market has a limited future!

A client is a retailer operating in a niche environment governed by lease agreements that give them exclusivity in that environment. That makes them a very attractive proposition, but only to a limited number of acquirers who want to operate in their niche.

Supplier Dependency.

Do you have one supplier that is irreplaceable and counts for a great deal of your business? That is a potential problem. There may be exceptions, where the supplier is so large and dominant the danger is minimal.

Being dependent upon Microsoft because you are a gold partner is one thing, but a client had developed products using a particular integrated circuit from a niche supplier. The supplier collapsed and my client had to fund a purchase of exceptional levels of inventory and commence a product re-design with an alternative chipset from a mass market supplier.

Products / Services.

Where in the life cycle is your product or service? If there are only a few years of useful life left, that will be unattractive. If it is not an established product, with a decent track record of sales, that too is a risk for the buyer

There are many examples of businesses where they have reached the end of the life-cycle, often because the product or service has been overtaken by market changes. If that is the case for your business you must either find a new market, or a new niche to serve.

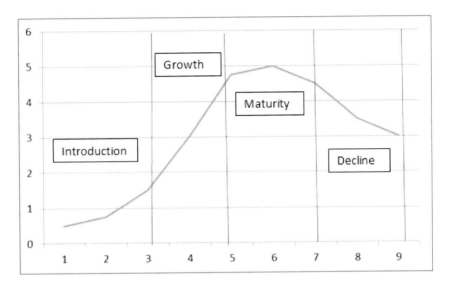

A good example here is the company St Ives Group, who were founded in 1964 as a sheet fed printing business. As the print market changed, St Ives acquired business to serve the book and magazine market. As those markets were disrupted, St Ives moved into marketing consultancy and more recently into digital marketing.

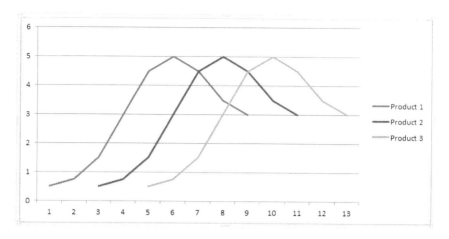

St Ives has new products (services) to replace those that were reaching the end of their life-cycle.

Management Team.

Do you have a well-rounded, established management team?

Many owner managers' struggle with and work around the deficiencies in their teams, sometimes hampered by the extensive history between the individuals and fear of upsetting or hurting the friends who are part of the team. That is fine in the short term, but longer term these challenges need to be overcome.

Two current clients come to mind in dealing with this. One is a substantial business dealing with multi-million pound contracts, where a senior manager is known in the business as "one-job-Bob" and the other is a much smaller business where the key operations person is a single mother, emotionally fragile, who has worked for the owners for more than 20 years. She insists in being involved in every step of the process, to the point where she will not take a vacation. In both cases, the individuals are hampering the growth and reducing the attractiveness of the business. One-job has a new trainee to develop and train; the operations lady has a large whiteboard listing all the activities that must be completed so that other team members can step in and help.

If you have to make changes to the management team, allow time for the new team to "bed in" and prove their capabilities. Remember that the buyers will look at the most recent years; if there's a change in management in that period it will raise doubts.

Ownership.

Are there are only a few shareholders to deal with? The rule here is the simpler the better, it is much easier than dealing with hundreds.

The owner of a business I advised had agreed a sale with the acquirer, but many years before had bought the business with the assistance of a venture capital partner. He had bought out their stake a few years later, but although the companies' house records reflected this, the company statutory records were incomplete. We were eventually able to complete the sale but only after some considerable heartache.

Minority shareholders have few rights, but it is still worthwhile investing in a shareholder agreement to pre-empt any future problems.

Intellectual Property.

Does the business own the IP, or is it in the hands of the owner? Worse still, does the IP belong to that contract developer you hired a few years ago?

Typically, intellectual property belongs to the creator. If you hire an author or a software developer, the material they create will belong to them – unless you have a contract to over-ride that.

Customer longevity.

Are you continually adding new customers? Are you losing customers and having to replace them? Businesses with long term customers, ideally underpinned with long term contracts are more valuable.

I have worked with a number of business owners who have repeat business as part of their model. The customers will come back to them time and time again. In most cases, it is a relatively small step to move those customers onto a contract securing the future revenue, but it is a massive change in the perception of the business and of its attractiveness in the marketplace.

Production Capability

The buyers of your business will (probably) be buying for the future profits they can make from your business. That means that any barriers to recreating and increasing those profits reduce the attractiveness of the business.

All businesses grow in steps, not a smooth curve. If you think of a manufacturing business, that's obvious. Moving from one shift to many or from one production line to many is an obvious step change, but step changes exist and occur in almost every business.

If the buyer will have to invest in replacement plant and machinery because what you have is at the end of its useful life that will reduce the amount they are prepared to pay.

Marketing Capability.

If you have a track record of successful marketing campaigns that have launched products or services and have generated new prospects, that is of real value to a buyer. They can see what has worked in the past and will know that they can replicate the campaign and expect to win new business.

If your marketing has been ad-hoc and poorly measured, the buyer has no such reassurance.

If your website has generated business and leads, that too will be welcomed by the buyer.

Sales Capability.

Marketing activities generate prospects, but sales activity converts prospects into customers.

Do you have a tried and trusted route to convert a prospect into a customer, or is it left to the individual sales person?

My florist client has a series of steps to convert the prospect through to the customer. We've documented these, so that it does not have to be just the owner who follows up on the prospect. Letters and emails have standard text – why re-invent the wheel or fix what is not broken.

Technology.

Technology can be fundamental to any business, and for the acquirer can be make or break. If the only way they can get at the information about your business is laborious and time consuming that will make the integration of your business much more difficult.

One business I worked with used software specifically written for their industry, many years ago. They'd worked with it for a number of years and had it customized to meet their needs. The operating system it ran on was obsolete, and the system could not be enhanced or enabled for the internet. The only option was a complete new system; had we been attempting to sell the business that would have reduced the price, if not caused the sale to fail altogether.

Strategy.

Is your strategy clear and consistent, or have you altered direction recently? If you are on a new course, what assurance the buyer will have that it is a valid strategy leading to success?

A new client who is an installations and maintenance business has launched a new ecommerce website to attract trade sales of products. The most likely buyers are his from the website are his competitors who will be buying at low margins. This is a strategy that does not make sense to me when he should be focused on building up his maintenance income stream.

Brand.

Is your brand known in your market place and have you protected the brand? Is the brand name a reason for an acquirer to buy your business?

Brands can have immense value and in the consumer world their effect can be seen every day. In the owner managed sector, one requirement is to separate the value of the brand from the individual. A business that is "Charlie Mullins" has little value; Pimlico Plumbers is the brand that Charlie has built, and the business spends considerable time and money on the presentation and image of the brand.

Premises.

The buyer is not buying your premises, they are buying the business. If the premises are owned by the business, arrange a sale (to the owner's pension fund?) and lease the premises on commercial terms, but with break clauses to give the buyer freedom of movement. If the premises are leased, make sure there is sufficient life in the lease for the buyer to be able to complete the deal and consider the integration, but on the other hand also make sure there are break clauses available. If the lease term is nearly up, consider short term (6 month / 1 year) extensions.

Several clients have transferred premises from the business to the pension fund to facilitate the sale of the business. The buyer is not buying the property, but the business. The property just becomes another asset to be financed by the buyer.

Financial efficiency.

Do you manage your working capital efficiently? Do you have a good debtor book, look after your assets and minimise the amount of capital tied up in the business?

If you have an extended debtor book, the buyer will probably discount a proportion of it to protect themselves from uncollectable. If the cash is in the bank, there can be no argument.

When you look at a debtor (receivables) report, the older the debt, the less likely it is that you can collect it. If you are buying those debts, you are unlikely to pay full price for old debts.

Final sale preparations.

In the last few months before taking the business to market, consider the payback periods on your decisions. If it seems likely that an investment will not have generated a return before you go to market, defer the investment. Save the cash and let the buyers make that decision and take that risk.

If there's a new product to be launched, is there enough time to see it established in the marketplace or should that launch be deferred and/or left to the new owner. You do not want to incur the launch costs and fail to receive sufficient revenues, simply because you have sold the business in the interim.

Consider reducing overhead to a minimum. If you can show that the business can be operated with a lower cost base, that will generate additional cash in the run up to the sale and the buyer will see a more profitable business.

If the company is holding excess or obsolete inventories, get rid of them. It is false economy to preserve them on the balance sheet, as the prudent purchaser will certainly uncover the true asset value, leaving the current owner with all the pain and no gain.

One of my clients was a hoarder by nature, and in his business had inventory of electronic components that were obsolete and no longer available. They were held to enable the repair of machinery built years before, and a few components were used each year. The owner carried this inventory at cost, even though at current consumption rates he had several years supply. The buyer wrote down the value of this inventory and spent even more time and effort reviewing the other inventory classes.

Clean up & run the accounts for the seller. It is quite usual for a set of accounts to be adjusted for the valuation of the business, but in the actual sale process those adjustments will be challenged by the buyers. If you can minimize the number and the value of those adjustments in the years prior to sale that will make the sale process much smoother.

A business owner wished to sell one of the three divisions of his business. The divisions shared premises, back-office costs, marketing and sales costs. The finance team created separate accounts for the divisions and implemented cross charging for the shared expenses. The prospective buyer was able to see the performance of the business as a stand-alone unit.

Slim down the balance sheet. It may well be that there are assets on the balance sheet no longer used by the business, or perhaps used by a different part of the business that is not included in the sale. Remove anything that is not part of the business being sold, and make sure what is being sold has a fair valuation.

Don't pay out your cash as dividends in the run up to a deal. In the UK, the vendor is likely to be eligible for entrepreneurs' relief and the sale proceeds taxed at just 10%. "Free" cash can be added to the agreed sale value and will qualify for the reduced tax rate. Do take tax advice – I am not a tax expert and there are a number of parameters surrounding any tax planning. Too much cash may make your business an investment business – so you won't get the reduced tax rate.

Make your reward systems contractual. As the sale process reaches fruition, there is likely to be a period when you agree with the preferred buyer that no exceptional transactions will take place. If you usually pay an end of year bonus, but it is not in the employment contract, you may not be able to make the payment without the approval of the buyer.

My client has two key employees, both of whom are board directors and minor shareholders. He feels that one of the employees has contributed far more to the success of the business than the other, but both have the same shareholding. My client would like to give an exceptional bonus, but is prevented from doing so without the approval of the purchaser.

Consider the real worth of your team. Over many years, it not unusual for employees with long and consistent service to receive annual increments that makes their package excessive. You may find that they are overpaid when you compare their package to the market value for the role they fulfil. You may want to offer them a generous retirement settlement and bring in new blood at a cheaper rate.

Invest in management information systems. A well run business will be able to produce timely, accurate and relevant detailed information. If it takes time to access information, or the information is stored in the vendor's head, it will be difficult to prove to the buyer that there are no black holes or skeletons. You will have to produce real detail in the due diligence phase of the transaction, but if you can show that it is readily available you will give the buyer much greater comfort.

My clients are a husband and wife team, running a lean business with little assistance in the financial accounting department. We are now in the early stages of Due Diligence, with a request for further disclosure. The finance manager is off ill and the external accountant will be tied up with tax returns for the next 2-3 weeks, so we are investing in interim management to make sure we provide information in a timely manner.

Settle any outstanding legal claims. There are few things more likely to disturb the equanimity of a buyer than the prospect of legal action, whether the claim is from a disgruntled former employee or a dissatisfied customer. Most claims can be settled through negotiation or arbitration, and it is far better to avoid uncertainty even if you believe the claim is without real merit.

Tidy up, clean up & polish. First impressions mean a lot, so if your offices are untidy or scruffy, or the workshop is a bit of a mess, tidy up. It might be worth a few hundred pounds on a lick of paint & a bit of carpet to improve those first impressions. Just imagine you mother is coming to visit!

I see a lot of different businesses over the course of a year. Those first impressions can be hard to shake, but even after discounting those I cannot recall a well-run business that operated from untidy or dirty premises. There are plenty that don't spend a fortune on premises, but they are clean and tidy.

Consider the environmental legacies. One of the highest levels of liability surrounds environmental contamination; if you operate a "dirty" business then you need to be seen to have addressed all environmental issues prior to sale.

A few years ago I was invited to value, prior to sale, a business that used various chemical processes in manufacturing accessories for machine tools. The owner took me on a tour of the premises, past open tanks of chemicals and through narrow passages between workshop sections. I am sure the chemical in the open tanks were harmless, but I know that dangerous chemicals were in use on site. The overall impression left me feeling that corners had been cut.

Consider the tax positions of all sides. Taxation in a corporate transaction requires a specialist advisor, and you would be well advised to take such advice well before you commence the sale process. Generally, the buyer will want to buy the assets of the business, leaving behind any historic liabilities that may be present, but this is disadvantageous for the vendor, who will be better served by a sale of shares.

Make sure you are compliant with all your statutory records, from the company register and minute book through to the employment contracts. Any areas of non-compliance will, at the least, require you to provide the buyer with a warranty and indemnity.

We were in the closing stages of a deal and the buyer's lawyer reviewed the shareholders register. Many years earlier, when my client bought the business, he had partnered with a Venture Capital company. He bought them out after a few years, and the transaction was correctly recorded at Companys House but incorrectly entered in the register. The legal position was that the VC was still a shareholder; we managed eventually to track down documentation that supported the redemption of their shares, but it was an uncomfortable few days for all.

Choose the right buyer or buyers. It is possible that your business is better sold in pieces, rather than in one piece, but whoever is the buyer the best value and the greatest likelihood of completion will come from a buyer with a good strategic reason to buy your business. That is usually the opportunity to sell your products and services to their clients or vice-versa. A good corporate finance advisor will be able to determine suitable candidates to approach.

Early in my career I had one client that had developed machinery used in the pharmaceutical industry and a second set of products used in the food industry. They shared some commonality in that they both had electronic control units with software developed in-house, but the markets were so disparate that marketing the business was challenging. With hindsight, we might have been better off splitting the business prior to sale.

Choosing the best deal.

Once the business has been marketed by an expert advisor, you should have two or more interested parties in a position to make indicative offers. Once the buyers have been vetted for their financial ability to complete the deal, one offer should be selected to become the preferred bidder.

It is not unusual for an offer to be a mix of cash, deferred payments, perhaps some payment contingent upon performance and even some shareholding in the combined business.

I differentiate between deferred payments and earn-outs; for me a deferred payment is either not contingent upon performance, or the performance hurdles are very low and/or within the control of the vendor. An example was a deferred payment that was contingent on the vendor introducing the acquirer to the top 80% of his customers, post-acquisition. Earn-outs are tied to performance hurdles that may or may not be reached. I prefer when possible to use Gross Margin as the metric; profits are too easily manipulated and revenue based targets can be dangerous.

Choosing which offer to select will be more a matter of personal preference than cold hard facts. Some offers will be obviously not good enough, but in a competitive situation it is likely that more than one will be at a very similar level. It is important to bear in mind that the vendors will have to work with the buyers for a number of weeks leading up to the completion of the deal, and then for a period thereafter, often stretching into months.

When the vendor contemplates the prospect of working with the various buyers, the choice can become clear very quickly.

Earn outs have an appalling reputation, but are sometimes necessary to close the gap between the value perceived by the buyer, who is of course fearful of over-paying and operating from a position of imperfect knowledge, and the value the seller places on his business. This is especially true where the forecast performance of the business is considerably above the current performance.

When I am advising on a sale, I look to secure as much as possible in the initial payment and a very small amount in deferred consideration. If an earn-out is necessary, then I will look to make it short-term (one year maximum) and linked to something that cannot easily be manipulated. That might be gross margins, or perhaps (as in the deal I am working on now) it might be the conversion value of open bids. My client has the inside knowledge to be pretty sure of some large deals; the buyer would be happy to pay more if he had the same certainty, but the deals will not close before the transaction is completed.

No surprises.

If the buyer is surprised at any stage, but especially in the latter stages of the negotiations, they will not take kindly to it. If there's something you have not disclosed, or something you want to keep, or an employee who requires special treatment, you need to disclose it early on in the process. It can be enough to tip the balance and cause a buyer to walk away.

Deal Fever

Look out for deal fever. The sale purchase of a business is an extraordinarily emotional event, especially for the first time vendor. It is easy to get caught up in the emotion, and make decisions or even remarks that are "out of character". A good business advisor can be the sounding board and the buffer that prevents emotions getting out of hand, enabling both sides to release the emotions without damaging the on-going relationship.

Conclusion

Not many private companies sell successfully, let alone sell at a premium. In many cases that's because there has been no thought given to what the potential purchaser wants or needs.

Every business I see has room for improvement, to make the business more marketable. Some of the changes required are minimal, and will have little impact on the day to day operation of the business, but some are a fundamental transformation of the businesses approach to its customers or marketplace.

The starting point is an assessment of your current position, and the identification of the value drivers and value drainers. Once you know where you are, you can develop a plan to build upon the value drivers and eliminate or at least significant reduce the value drainers.

There is more information on value drivers and value drivers in the next chapter.

3 WHAT'S A BUSINESS WORTH?

The answer to that question may well depend upon who is asking.

Valuation is often described as an art form, not a science. It might help to think of the value as a hologram – it changes as you look at it from different angles, and under different circumstances.

In most cases, there will be 3 separate views of the value of a business.

The first will be the view of the owner, well aware of all the features and characteristics of the business but equally emotionally involved and perhaps with rose tinted glasses helping them overlook some of the negative factors.

The second will be the view of the buyer or investor. They are also likely to have an emotional reaction and in this case fear and caution will be dominant. They know very little about the business, and are fearful that their investment will be at risk.

The third valuation is that of the market – it is most likely to be a blend of the first two.

Valuation for sale.

Value, like beauty, is in the eye of the beholder.

A business that has immense value to one potential buyer may have very little value, or attraction, to another.

Red or Blue?

Your business manufactures and sells blue widgets. Your competition only has red widgets.

If the prospective buyer doesn't care what colour the widget is, the two businesses can be directly compared, but if the buyer only wants blue widgets, your business is worth far more than the manufacturer of red widgets!

Your business may be your life's work and you are passionate about it, but when it is time to sell, your passion and your past efforts have very little to do with the value a buyer will place on it.

The over-riding principle is that in 90% of cases a business is bought for the future profits it will make, and the valuation calculation is an attempt to place a value on those future profits.

The other 10% of business purchases are for bought for lifestyle choices, a passion or an interest (think football clubs) or for egotistical purposes.

Your unique selling proposition will influence the buyer to pay a little more for the business, especially if there is a first class strategic fit, but underlying everything is the financial performance of the business under your guidance.

There are many different technical tools and calculations used to try and estimate value, but the real challenge is to identify the right strategic buyer and see the business from their perspective.

Valuation to attract investors

There are other times within a business lifecycle when you will want a valuation, when the purpose is not a sale to a strategic acquirer but attracting an equity investor. In this case it's important to consider the business from the investors' perspective, including the level of risk and reward the investor face and the stage in the life of the business.

With early stage investors, it is important to consider what other benefits and/or features could be in the mix. It is often the case that Angel investors will re-invest in the sectors in which they made their money – so for example, a technology entrepreneur may more comfortable investing in a tech start-up than in a fashion retailer. From the investee's perspective, the Angel with a background in the same business space will bring a wealth of contacts, knowledge and experience that might short cut the path to growth.

Typically, an Angel investor is a wealthy individual willing to take higher risks in the expectation of higher rewards and their funding is in return for a stake in the business.

Valuation for incentive Schemes

If you want to give your key employees shares in the business, or perhaps grant them options you will need a valuation.

An option is a right to buy at a future date, and is usually at a fixed price; the recipient benefits from the increase in value between the date of grant and the exercise date.

The valuation will be required for the calculation of any tax liability due, and if you are taking advantage of the tax reductions offered by the government you will need to submit a valuation as part of the registration of the scheme.

Valuing a potential acquisition.

You may also wish to put a value on a business you want to acquire, but that valuation is as much about the negotiation and the approach as it is about a calculation. There will be a value to you – if this is a strategic acquisition, and you know that you can drive greater benefits from the combination of the businesses, you can model what those benefits might be and value those benefits. You'll also need to value the business as it would appear to other potential buyers – who do not have the synergies that you can derive – so that you can negotiate from a position of strength.

Market & Sector Conditions

Every calculation of value has to take into account the prevailing economic and market conditions. If the economy in which the business is operating is weak, then the values will necessarily be lower than if the economy is strong.

The market conditions probably have an even bigger influence; if a particular market is booming, businesses operating in that market will command higher values. If the market is in decline, the value will be considerably lower.

It is entirely possible that a change in the value of a business does not relate at all to the performance of the business, but to changes in the external conditions in which the business operates.

It's certainly true that valuations in 2010 were considerably below valuations achieved in 2006-7.

Sector and market conditions vary over time. A sector can be "hot" and achieving very high valuations (remember the dot com boom?) or cold and unfashionable so achieving low valuations. That is a reflection of the demand side of the supply and demand equation. If your sector is hot, and there are lots of buyers, you will achieve a better valuation. If your sector is less fashionable, the valuation will be lower.

Value Drivers and Value Drainers.

There are features and attributes of a business that add value, across all sectors and equally there are some that will reduce value if they exist in a business.

The larger the business, the higher the relative value will be. In the next section I talk about valuation methodologies, but no matter which method you apply the ratios used for a larger business are likely to be considerably higher than those applied to a smaller business.

A good track record will command greater value that one that is poor, or patchy. Remembering that the buyer or investor is purchasing the future profits of the business and that they will use the past performance as a guide to the future makes this obviously true.

Features that increase the likelihood of future performance, such as an extensive forward order book or contracted recurring revenues are extremely attractive to the buyer or investor.

Features that reduce the risk (or the perceived risk) of unexpected events or undisclosed information will help the buyer or investor gain confidence, and enable them to place a higher value on the business. Quality systems, audited accounts and similar third party validations fall into this category.

Almost every feature of a business should be examined from the buyers' perspective to see if its characteristics make it a *value driver*, or a *value drainer*.

The "Business Value" mind-map on the following two pages illustrates the areas I will discuss with the business owners when identifying the relevant characteristics of the business.

Tim Luscombe

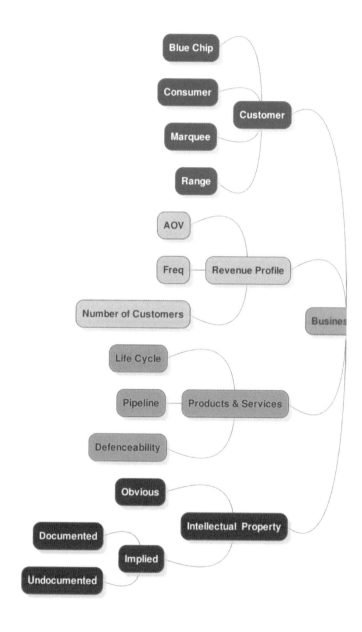

40

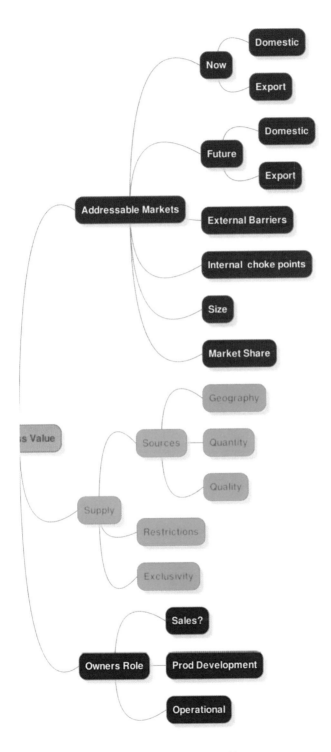

Ways to calculate a valuation.

In many sectors there is a rule of thumb that is known in the sector and can be used as a basis for valuation, but I have found the rule of thumb and other valuation methodologies tend to come out with much the same overall value.

If I am undertaking a valuation, I will use as many different techniques or calculations as I can; if there's a major discrepancy between the various methods, that is worthy of further investigation.

The valuation starts with the accounts, or financial statements, and will usually look at the last 3 years with more emphasis on the most recent year. If the business is being valued part way though a year, management information will be used in addition to the annual statements.

The accounts will need to be adjusted, or normalised, so that the business is directly comparable to others in the same sector. These adjustments will include the elimination of any truly exceptional (and therefore not repeatable) events.

It is very likely in private companies that the owner has managed the structure and the quantum of their drawings from the business to minimise taxation. The adjustment is to substitute the drawing of the owners, including any expenses that would not be incurred under new ownership, with market rate drawings for the job(s) the directors actually do.

The final set of adjustments is to remove the non-operating elements of the business. For example, a business may have built up excess cash, or perhaps is invested in property that is not in use by the business. These should be eliminated from the accounts, together with any income or expenditure, before the valuation methodologies are applied.

I did on one occasion receive an information pack from a corporate finance house that included a note in the accounts "Livestock classified as plant refers to a Racehorse" and needless to say we did not proceed with the purchase of the business – or the horse!

Very broadly, I classify valuation calculations or techniques into these groups.

Asset based valuations do pretty much what it says on the tin. There are a number of different calculations that take the value of assets as a starting point, including or excluding different classes of assets and perhaps applying some discount to stated values – for example, 85% of net receivables.

This form of valuation is often used when the business is to be liquidated, or in some other way will not continue as a trading business.

Cash-flow based valuations are often used by businesses seeking to fund their acquisition activities through debt finance. The "non-cash" elements of the profit and loss are removed to provide an indication of the underlying cash flow, which can of course be used to service debt. Capital expenditure, particularly in capital intensive businesses, will have a significant impact.

You may well hear about EBITDA (Earnings Before Interest Taxation Depreciation and Amortisation) in the context of this. EBITDA is a measure of the cash generated by a business – and hence of the debt that the business may be able to service.

Cash flow based valuation techniques often use the NPV (net present value) of future estimated cash-flows. This has the additional advantage of allowing a "Buy" strategy to be compared to a "Build" strategy. The same valuation technique can be used to value the acquisition and the costs & revenues of building the business organically.

Earnings based valuations are frequently used for private companies, with a publicly traded company in the same sector as a starting point. The underlying rationale is strong, as the publicly traded company has a value determined by the market and we can use ratios to estimate comparable values for the private company.

There are adjustments to make for size (a business turning over a few million will not command the same (apportioned) value as one turning over several hundred million and for lack of liquidity. It is not easy to dispose of your stake in a private company; there are probably only a few buyers, possibly only one.

My final group of valuations are probably the simplest and favoured in the private company market place for their simplicity. **Payback valuations** simply relate the value to the underlying earnings over a number of years – for example, a buyer may require a payback over 5 years.

Valuations in practice

Examples:

Valuing a company using an asset based methodology

Let us assume that the assets of the company are 1,500k.

Included in the assets are cash and property.

We need to exclude the "surplus" cash as that can either be bought on a like for like basis by the acquirer (which may have tax advantages) or taken as a dividend by the owners, prior to the sale.

Calculating the surplus cash requires a cash flow forecast, and will be a topic for negotiation, but in very simple terms it is the cash held by the business in excess of its working capital needs.

We also need to exclude the property as it will distort the valuation applied to the underlying business. I frequently advise my clients to move property from the company to their personal ownership – perhaps using a pension fund – so that any acquirer is not constrained by the need to fund the acquisition of the property, as well as the business. Once the property is in personal ownership, the company will need to rent it at commercial rates and terms.

In this case, if the property is in the balance sheet at 600k and the surplus cash is 400k, the remaining asset value is 500k.

We would value the business at 500k.

Valuing a company using a cash flow methodology.

Our private company makes a profit (from the published accounts) of 150k.

Our first step is to "normalise" the accounts. In this case it is clear that the Managing Director (and part owner) is paid 20k per annum. We expect that the market rate for the MD's job would be 80k.

We find that the company pays for club memberships, first class travel on business trips and makes a pension contribution for the MD. The club membership would not be renewed for an MD who was not also the owner, the pension contributions are excessive and business class travel would be expected.

We also find that the MD's partner is paid 20k per annum for working one day a week. This role could be absorbed into the workload of the team.

The adjusted profit is 172k

This business has the building, which is amortised at 5% per annum, and 500k of other assets that attract 25k depreciation.

Capital expenditure is forecast at 15k per annum for the next 3 years.

A rough estimate of cash flows would be:

172 + Building amortisation of 30 + depreciation of 25 = 227k less Capex of 15k = 212.

But if the building is to be transferred to the business owner and then leased:

$$212k - \text{building rent at } 50k = 162k$$

We can estimate that over the next 3 years the business will generate

162k in cash each year and a total of 486k.

The cash received in two years from an investment made now should be discounted to allow for the delay and lost opportunity; the opportunity to earn an income from these funds.

We use a Net Present Value calculation for this.

The NPV formula is
$$\frac{R_t}{(1+i)^t}$$

Where
t – the time of the cash flow
i – the discount rate (the rate of return that could be earned on an investment in the financial markets with similar risk.); the opportunity cost of capital
R_t – the net cash flow i.e. cash inflow – cash outflow, at time t.

Using a spreadsheet and a 5% discount rate, the cash flow of 197 per year for 3 years gives a NPV of 441k.

This result varies greatly; you may choose a 5 year period to consider cash flows, or perhaps a high or lower interest or discount rate.

An alternative to using the "lost opportunity" rate to choose your discount rate is to consider the cost of capital for your business.

The Weighted Average Cost of Capital of WACC is calculated by considering the cost of all forms of finance for the business.

Example:

A business has a long term bank loan of 100k at 7% per annum and one class of ordinary shares with an equity value of 350k. The dividend is set at 10%.

The WACC for this business would be

$$\frac{100 * 7\% + 350 * 10\%}{450} = \frac{42}{450} = 9.3\%$$

If you applied this discount rate to the NPV calculation as above, the resultant value is 408k.

Using the WACC has a number of advantages; the shareholders and the bank will expect to continue to receive their income and interest, so you need to ensure that whatever the investment, the returns earned will continue to support such payments.

You may consider EBITDA as the starting point for a cash flow based valuation, and there are several other methodologies you might apply.

Valuing a private company using a P/E Ratio.
Public or listed businesses are valued by supply and demand in the market, and we can use the ratios from those public businesses to try to reflect the relative strength or weakness of a sector.

If you were valuing a business in the construction sector, you would look at the valuation of a range of listed construction businesses. You would not look at technology or healthcare businesses.

The value of a public company is the sum of the quantity of shares issued multiplied by their individual value, and of course it varies from moment to moment as shares are bought and sold.

The key ratio we can derive for our private company valuations from the value of a public company is the price to earnings or P/E ratio.

This is calculated as the market price per share divided by the earnings per share (eps) and the eps is calculated by dividing the total post tax earnings of the public company by the number of shares.

A public company in the same sector has 5m shares, makes a profit of 1.2m and each share is valued at 3.00

Earnings per share are 1,200,000 / 5,000,000 or 0.24
The P/E ratio is 3.0 / 0.24 = 12.5

Unfortunately, you cannot just use that as a ratio for our private company. There will be a significant discount; each share of the public company has many potential buyers, but with a private company there will be far fewer – perhaps only one.

The public company will be much, much larger than the private company. Larger companies are more highly rated than smaller companies, so a discount is applicable. In this case the public company makes nearly ten times the profits of the private company.

Taking these factors into account, it is not unusual to discount the P/E ratio of a comparable public company by anything from 50 to 70% so that we might apply a P/E ratio of between 3.75 and 6.25 to our private company. This is the point at which the judgement of the corporate finance advisor comes into play – there is no hard and fast rule.

Our valuation could be between (172*3.75) 645k and (172*6.25) 1075k

Valuation using a Payback period

This is a very simplistic methodology and is often favoured in the private sector.

We take the adjusted, post-tax profits of the target business and multiply by the number of years we are prepared to wait to recover our money.

In our example above, the company makes 172k and we want payback in 3 years.

The value is 516k

Summary
Our various calculations have given us the following values:

Method	Low Value	High Value
Asset based	500k	
Cash flow.	441k	408k
P/E Ratio.	645k	1075k
Payback period	516k	

We have a lowest valuation of 441k and a highest valuation of 1075k, but brief inspection suggests the highest value is anomalous, so we should probably exclude it.

That leaves a range of 441k to 645k; we have an asset value of 500k confirming/supporting the lower end of the valuation range, so the premium over asset value is a maximum of 145k.

That premium is known as goodwill.
☐
The buyers' viewpoint
The next step when considering an acquisition is to estimate what the business you are buying will bring to the party.
We're only buying the business because we believe the whole will be greater

than the sum of the parts. We plan to generate more profit under our ownership than the business was making under the previous owner, perhaps by better purchasing or by cross selling products…there will be several different potential synergies.

Typically, you'll prepare a schedule like this one:

	Our Company		Target		Combined		Benefit	Planned	
Revenues	5,705		1,467		7,172		100	7,272	
Cost of Sales	3,423	60%	900	61%	4,323	60%	13	4,310	59%
Gross Profit	2,282	40%	567	39%	2,849	40%		2,962	41%
Operating Expenses	1,200	21%	348	24%	1,548	22%	50	1,498	21%
Operating Profit	1,082	19%	219	15%	1,301	18%	63	1,464	20%
Interest	7		4		11		2	9	
Profit before tax	1,075		215		1,290			1,455	
Taxation	215		43		258			291	
Profit after tax	860	15%	172	12%	1,032	14%		1,164	16%

The first 6 columns are the simple addition of the existing businesses and the resultant ratios.

The benefit column represents the post-acquisition benefits we believe we can derive; additional sales, some improvement in the target margins, some saving in operational costs etc.

From this we can see that if we achieve the benefits, the increase in annual profitability is

$$1,164-860=304$$

On the negative side, there will be a significant cost in the acquisition of the business, both in terms of professional advisors but also the often underestimated post acquisition integration costs.

Let's assume those costs amount to 100k.

Our calculated benefit over 3 years would be

$$304*3-100=812$$

This is significantly in excess of the values derived above from the analysis of the target company's figures and gives us a high level of comfort in proceeding with an offer.

Conclusion

Valuation is closer to an art form than it is to a science, and there is plenty of opportunity to make the valuation be whatever you want it to be!

It is invaluable to get an external view, from someone with experience and knowledge of the target company market place.

Those things that carry significant value to the business owner, the history and the emotional attachments probably carry very little value to the potential purchaser or investor. The investor or acquirer is looking forward, trying to see what the future holds and their only guide is the past.

Tim Luscombe

4 RAISING MONEY FOR YOUR BUSINESS

A fundamental principle of business is that successful businesses will generate cash-flow. Businesses that are at particular points of their life cycle may not generate enough cash for their needs, but over the long term successful businesses generate cash.

Funding and the life cycle.

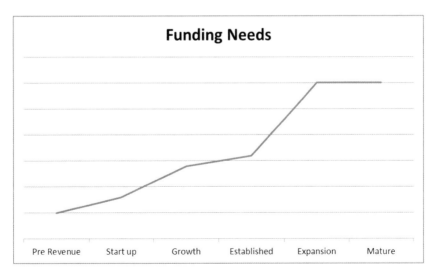

When considering what source and what type of funding your business needs, it's a good idea to refer back to the business life-cycle and determine where you are. Some forms of funding are not appropriate for some of the stages in the business.

In the early stages of a business funding is mostly from the 3F's: Friends, Family and Fools. There are some specialist funders, notably those attached to scientific or research institutions, providing funding through "incubators". Funding at this stage is most likely to be equity based, where the funder becomes a part owner of the business.

One significant marker in the business life-cycle is the generation of the first revenues, when the business has moved from a theoretical idea to a practical proposition, with a product or service that has been exchanged for money. The business is no longer "pre-revenue" and another set of funding options becomes available.

In this post revenue start-up phase, Angel investors play a large part. Typically, an Angel investor is a wealthy individual willing to take higher risks in the expectation of higher rewards and their funding is in return for a stake in the business.

It's also at this stage that the first opportunities for funding though debt become available. Lenders can see there is a track record, and with a forecast or a business plan can see how the business may be able to "service" the debt (that's banker speak for be able to pay the interest) and over time be able to repay the debt. The big difference is that debt funders do not take an equity stake in the business.

When the business enters the growth phase, it is generating cash (but not enough to finance the growth) and has a track record. That gives confidence to lenders and equity investors that the business can succeed and is a lower risk.

Debt and Equity will be cheaper.

At this point the business will have some assets; perhaps some customers who owe money (debtors, or receivables) and some forms of asset based lending become available.

Established businesses have all the options available to them as they have the asset base, the track record and the stability to reassure investors and lenders. Businesses at this stage of the life cycle should only be borrowing for specific purposes, not from general need.

Business in the expansion phase can equally access most kinds of funding; many business that expand through acquisition will use some form of asset based lending to fund the purchase, with a view to paying down those loans within a relatively short period.

A characteristic of a mature business is that it is generating cash in excess of its needs; in public companies this phase of the life cycle is often accompanied by increases in dividends or even share buy-backs.

Funding Types

Very broadly, funding can be defined as debt, equity and grant or donation

Debt is a loan or loans, including overdrafts, hire purchase, leasing, mortgages etc. that will be repaid at some point in the future and attract interest.
Amongst the many forms of debt finance are the Enterprise Finance Guarantee loans which are partly guaranteed by the government and are aimed at businesses less than 5 years old. They carry an insurance premium of 2%.

Bank loans and overdrafts are very common for businesses that are established, but there's usually a requirement for security in the form of charges (debentures) over the business assets, and often with directors' guarantees and even personal guarantees.

Asset financing is usually used to finance the acquisition of new plant and equipment, but can also be used to alter the financial structure of a business, for example using asset financing against owned assets to release funds for other purposes.

Invoicing financing is becoming more and more popular. This is where the finance provider will lend a proportion (often as much as 75%) of the amount you are owed by your customers. New entrants to the market allow you to finance single invoices, rather than the whole debtor book.

Equity is the ownership of the business. The equity provider receives a proportion of the ownership of the business, and is entitled to share in the profits of the business. The proportion of shares owned by each investor, and their rights are determined by the type of share (In the US they refer to Stock) that the investor holds.

Most companies have only "ordinary" shares where all shares are equal, but there is almost no limit to the number of different groups or classes of shares that can be created.

One reason for creating different groups of shares may be voting rights; in the end, the shareholders control the company (and appoint directors) so it is possible to create a structure where the majority ownership of the business is with one group of shares, but the control (through voting rights) is with another group or class of shares.

A second reason for a different class of shares maybe different financial terms; often preference shares are created to provide a greater income stream for the preference share holder.

There's a wide variety of possible share types and classes; in the end the rights of each class are determined by the articles of association of the company.
There are also various hybrid types of funding that share some of the characteristics of both debt and equity; mezzanine financing is a loan that can be converted into equity under certain conditions, Redeemable preference shares can or may be repaid under certain conditions.

Grant funding is usually funding for a specific project or operation. The source of funds is most often a government or social enterprise, with objectives to assist businesses with their projects that meet their criteria. An example is the Technology Strategy Board, which provides funding to businesses that are investing in innovative technology. You can also get grants for some projects within the business, notably Growth Accelerator and the Manufacturing Advisory Service.

Donations are similar to grants, but are one of the features from the new models of crowd sourced funding, where money is donated to a business (or cause). In many cases the donor receives some form of acknowledgement in the form of a reward, for example a beta copy of the game they have helped to fund.

Funding Sources.

Public companies, able to access a recognised market for their equity, have a model of raising funds from a large numbers of shareholders who can buy and sell their holding relatively freely. Many public companies can access debt finance in a similar way, by issuing bonds.

The traditional funding model for private companies has by contrast always been relatively large investments from relatively few sources, so that a private company with more than a handful of shareholders is unusual.

New entrants to the funding market are providing some much needed stimulus and using some very different models.

Crowd funding is becoming more prevalent, where the model is the aggregation of many smaller investment amounts enabling businesses (and charitable causes) to raise funds from lots of small investors. Businesses that have had most success with this model are those that have a mass-market appeal, or those that appeal to a particular niche.

A computer games company seeking to raise funds for the next generation of a popular game might well resort to crowd-funding, rewarding these early-stage investors with a beta-copy of the game. Not only does the business raise the necessary funding, it also receives feedback on the beta release enabling improvement to the final version of the game.

In a similar vein, peer to peer lending platforms are aggregating many small investments to meet funding needs.

Where to find Equity finance.
Incubators funds are usually attached to a geographic location, such as a university or science park, and are well signposted and known in the area.
Angel investors are usually high net worth individuals who have an interest in a particular market sector, where they may have extensive experience and knowledge. That experience allows them to assess high risk opportunities, and they may choose to contribute to the management of the business. Most business angels operate though clubs or networks, and there may well be some filtering before you have the opportunity to present.
Venture Capital investors will only consider larger investments, typically above £1m, and as with angel investors may well be sector specific. You will usually find the investment criteria for projects they will consider listed on their websites, but as always a personal introduction is more likely to succeed than a cold approach through the website.

Where to find Debt Finance.
There are many sources of debt finance, ranging from the high street banks through to the peer to peer lending platforms.
Asset based finance, in particular, has an almost unlimited range of finance providers. Often manufacturers of particular plant or equipment will have a

funding package available to the potential buyer to make the purchase easier. It is always wise to compare the terms on offer as this is a very competitive market.

A subset of asset based finance is invoice finance, where funding is secured upon the invoices you raise to your customers. You may have heard of this as "factoring" but there are many terms in use for essentially the same model.

This should be used with care; it is not a solution to the on-going finance needs of the business as it must be repaid. This form of finance provides a one-time boost, and can be used to resolve a short term funding crisis. Businesses undergoing exceptional growth can use invoice finance to help fund that growth.

Crowd funding for debt is becoming well established and is very effective. Decisions are made quickly and interest rates are very competitive.

Making your case for investment.

If you are seeking investment, don't lose sight of the fact that it is more than just the facts and figures. Any investor is taking a risk and the higher the risk the higher the reward they will seek. That higher reward comes from the business, and the financing is therefore more expensive. It's important that you are passionate about the business, but you must balance that with a healthy dose of realism.

Some things to bear in mind.

You are selling, not buying, when you raise finance. You are exchanging your investment opportunity in return for the investors' money, in the same way you would exchange your goods or services for your customers' money.

This is your plan, they are your numbers not your accountants or your Finance Director's. All too often we see or hear business owners unable to answer fundamental questions about their plan, and indeed I have heard a business owner say "I don't know where that comes from, my accountant did that for me"

You may want to conquer the world, but there might be a few smaller steps that you can take first. If you are over ambitious, you increase the perceived risk and reduce your chances of getting funding. If you do get funding, it will be more expensive. Have the big picture, the global ambition on show, but go after funding for the little steps. Many businesses go through several rounds of funding, often with different investors, as they move along the life-cycle.

A forecast with a sudden leap in revenues or profits is not likely to be accepted. It may be that new product features or a new market launch support the forecast but it is much more likely that the revenues and profits will be an extension of the past, not a great leap forward.

A good management team will fix a poor product or service; a poor management team will fail to make the best of an excellent opportunity. Look at your team from the outside; how strong is the track record, and what strengths and weaknesses do you have? If you know you have a weakness in the team, plan to strengthen the team. It may be the investors have the knowledge, or more likely the contacts, to be able to help.

Investors are risk averse. They may make fantastic returns from their investments, but one loss takes a lot of wins to recover. How much comfort you can provide? How unlikely is it that their entire investment will be lost?

Investors will have a defined set of criteria for their investments. Those might be size, sector specific, life-cycle stage, geography…there are any number. Make sure that your business and investment needs meet the criteria or you will be wasting your and the investor's time.

Don't hide anything; there a very good chance that anything you try to hide will be uncovered prior to the investment, and if that's not the case and it comes to light afterwards you will have a very poor relationship. Be honest and open, build the relationship.

Investors will want to see that you are focused on the business and "have some skin in the game". If you have other business interests you will need to satisfy their concern that you are paying enough attention to the business they are investing in. How much will it hurt you if it doesn't succeed?

There's no substitute for preparation and an investment in an advisor and time to rehearse your pitch is likely to be repaid many times over. You will probably only get one chance to pitch.

Every investor will want their return on investment, and at some point will want their money back – an exit. That is likely to be within 3 to 5 years, and your plan and presentation need to include the exit.

As you write up your pitch, make sure you are meeting the investor's needs. You will be passionate about your product, your service, your business but the investor is not. They want their questions answered; so make sure you know what the questions are – they don't want to hear what you want to talk about!

There's a very good chance the investors have not read the business plan in detail. They'll read the exec summary (see below) and then they will dip in and out of the plan. Don't assume they've read anything or know anything about your business, they've probably "read" another 50 plans since yours.

The executive summary is crucial. It won't get you funding, but it might get your proposal filed in the waste basket. Make sure your unique, defensible proposition is clearly set out in the exec summary its job is to get them to read further.

Consider your proposals from the investors' point of view, and make sure they qualify, wherever possible, for tax breaks. Although tax allowances will probably not be the driving reason for investment, they can be the difference between your opportunity and the alternatives. In the UK, the most relevant are the EIS and SEIS schemes.

Make it easy for the investors; put your contact details and your website on the front page of the plan; leave out the technical jargon and the acronyms and keep it in plain English

The plan is much more than numbers, or a product & market positioning statement. Investors will want to know how you are going to run the business.

What's your USP? You need to outline, in just a couple of sentences, why your business is different and why your customers chose to do business with you rather than the competition. Be very clear that these are not sufficient:

1. Quality of service
2. Very / extremely professional
3. Passionate about x
4. A people business
5. Work with you not for you
6. Committed
7. Pro-active
8. Good value for money
9. Very / extremely reliable

Test your USP statement by putting your close competitors name in place of your own. If the statement is still true, you haven't created a USP.

Investors will be interested in how you intend to capture prospects, how your marketing activity will work, and what others are doing in the marketplace. Systems and processes for marketing will encourage investors but reliance upon the genius of an individual will not.

Once you've captured the prospect, how are you going to turn them into a customer? It's that process that holds the value, not the efforts of the superstar salesman.

When you've done business with the customer for the first time, how will you connect with them again & gain repeat business? Repeat business is very attractive to an investor, and recurring revenues are even more so. A business that covers its costs through recurring revenue is very attractive indeed.

The cost of funding.
Whatever form of finance you seek, it has a cost to the business. That cost is the reward to the funder, and it's important to recognise all the costs and compare carefully across the different sources of funds that are available to you. Don't omit any setup or arrangement fees from the calculations.

It may be that a source of funds will cost you an annual rate of 12%, but the project you are considering will only generate a 10% return.

Equity funding also carries a cost to the business – most obviously in the dividends paid to shareholders, but equally in the capital return received when the shareholder exits.
Your cheapest source of funding is always within the business, through managing your working capital.

Taking a simple example, a business turns over £12m and makes a gross margin of 50%. It pays its suppliers on 30 days, holds 3 months inventory and has debtor days of 90.

A simple working capital calculation looks like this

Business Turnover		£	12,000,000
Debtor Days			90
Debtor Value	Approx	£	3,000,000
Cost of Sales			50%
Payable days			30
Creditor Value		£	500,000
Inventory Holding			90
Inventory Value		£	1,500,000
Working Capital		£	4,000,000

The working capital is calculated by adding the debtor value to the inventory value and subtracting the creditor value.

If that same business were able to make some changes, so that suppliers are paid on 60 day terms, it only holds one months' inventory and improves its debtor days to 30 the resultant working capital calculation is:

Business Turnover		£	12,000,000
Debtor Days			30
Debtor Value	Approx	£	1,000,000
Cost of Sales			50%
Payable days			60
Creditor Value		£	1,000,000
Inventory Holding			30
Inventory Value		£	500,000
Working Capital		£	500,000

So that is a release of £3.5m in cash to a business that only turns over £12m.

The numbers are crude and you may be thinking this is unrealistic, but in the real world I took responsibility for the finances of a distribution business with sales of approximately £30m. Debtor days were 90, creditors were always paid exactly at 30 days (a point of pride for the management) and we held significant inventory.

The (public) parent company promoted the "free cash" the business generated at each quarterly set of results and had set a target for debtor days in this business of 57.

We worked to reduce inventory holdings – mostly through supply agreements where we knew we could get product within defined timescales, so we were able to apply just in time methodologies.

We also re-negotiated many of the supplier payment terms, with particular focus on our larger suppliers. Some suppliers were also customers, where the debtor days were in the 60-90 region but we were still paying them at 30 days.

The most effort and emphasis went into collecting from our customers. The debtor days of 90 were actually flattering – we did significant business on credit cards – and were able to reduce debtor days from 90 to 28. Don't accept what you are told is "reasonable" without checking the assumptions!

The results in that business were:

Business Turnover	£ 30,000,000	£ 30,000,000
Debtor Days	90	28
Debtor Value	£ 7,500,000	£ 2,500,000
Cost of Sales	50%	50%
Payable days	30	60
Creditor Value	£ 1,250,000	£ 2,500,000
Inventory Holding	90	30
Inventory Value	£ 3,750,000	£ 1,250,000
Working Capital	£ 10,000,000	£ 1,250,000
Capital Released		£ 8,750,000

A word of warning here; in many industries it is common to offer prompt payment, or prompt settlement discounts, often in the range of 2% or even more. This is expensive funding at 27% APR!

It's often the case that customers will take the settlement discount, even when they make the payment late. If that's something you have to offer, because of your industry or sector, consider offering a retrospective discount through a credit note at the end of the quarter. At least you can enforce the prompt payment. Model the business as though the sale were net of the settlement discount, so that if it is not taken you have some upside surprise.

5 BUYING THE BUSINESS YOU WORK IN.

Many people dream of running their own business and sometimes you'll be in a position to think about buying the business you work in.

There are many circumstances where an MBO might be appropriate, from a private business owner considering an exit through to a larger business considering the disposal of a division that is no longer core to their strategy.

Most MBO companies do better than their peers and better than they performed under the old owner. That's not really surprising, as now the management team are more than just employees – they are committed to the business. It's important to realise that this is a long term investment; your money will be tied up for a number of years. It is very likely you will have to pay down debt and perhaps pay off a financial investor before you can start to draw dividends. That might be 5 years.

If you are successful in buying the business, that's just the start. Do you have the skills, knowledge and experience to successfully run the business? One way to think about that is to write down all the functions, then assign names to them from your team. You might want to get the existing owner to do the same thing; there may be some surprises for you!

Do a SWOT analysis on your team; be prepared to hire the skills you don't have in-house. You may find that you don't have the resources and skills to make a success of the business, but that can be more than a recruitment exercise. You may be able to find someone who wants to invest, or buy-in to the business, in a deal that is known as a Buy-In, Management Buy Out or BIMBO.

The Private Seller

As an employee, working for the owner, you have an established relationship. If you are going to make an approach to buy the business, you will change that relationship. There's a risk that if you make an approach, and it does not work out (for whatever reason) you will not be able to continue in your role.

To minimise this risk, make the approach very carefully and be as subtle as you can. Be prepared to take your time and give the owner time to adapt to your suggestion.

Money matters. The chances are that you cannot pay as much for the business as a third party, with deeper pockets, can afford. You may need to seek a financial partner, either through debt financing (MBO type deals are very popular with banks and asset finance houses) or, for the larger business, through an equity participation.

It is very important to correctly plan the business and ensure you have sufficient finance available to ride out any rocky patches along the way. Don't forget that in adding to the debt burden of the company you are weakening the balance sheet, leaving the business more exposed to potential hazards.

You will also need money to further develop the business. Expansion and growth require additional working capital; new products and new markets take time to mature a produce a return.

Be open with the exiting owner about your finances, and be prepared to go "all-in"

If you do bring on board a financial partner they are very likely to have priorities that differ from yours. That is especially true of an equity investor, who will most likely to expecting an exit over a 3 to 5 year time scale.

For the existing owner, there are a number of benefits to selling to the team and you'll need to emphasise them. You probably cannot compete on price, so compete on the emotional appeal of looking after the business and the team. There's also the avoidance of a protracted sale process involved in the sale to a trade buyer.

Get Help. Negotiating the deal can be very time consuming, and as mentioned above emotions can run very high. In the meantime, you've got a job, and a business that requires your attention on a day to day basis.

Many businesses suffer a fall-off in performance during a deal, let alone a MBO. The management team are distracted from the day to day operations whilst they are busy negotiating a deal – and the effect is amplified when the management team are sitting on opposite sides of the table.

Who is left to steer the business, and will there be a business left to come back to when the deal is done?

It is a really good idea for both the existing owner and the MBO team to appoint a good corporate finance advisor and focus on keeping the business going.

There may be more sources of funds available than you realise, and the conversations with the owner may be more fruitful if both sides can express opinions untainted by the (probably many years) experience of working together.

The two finance advisors will take instructions from the vendor and the MBO team, and then sit together to work out a deal.

Structuring the deal. Many MBO's are partly financed by the vendor who will take payment over time, reducing the need for the management team to raise debt and/or equity funding.

There's often the possibility of refinancing assets.

I worked with the manager of a tour coach business where we raised a good proportion of the purchase price by refinancing the coaches from 3 to 5 year arrangements.

Commonly you will see other assets of the business leveraged to provide a proportion of the purchase price.

It is not at all unusual for a new company to be formed to undertake the acquisition, purchasing the assets or the shares of the existing business so that the new ownership structure can be clearly established from the outset.

External equity backers often have a key role in the MBO, but one of the challenges is that they will need an exit route. Financial backers are likely to want to exit within a 3 to 5 year time frame, which may be much shorter than the management team would like.

The exit for a financial backer may take many forms:
• Trade sale – selling the business to another business
• Secondary buy-out – selling the equity stake to another financial investor
• Initial Public Offering or flotation – selling shares on the stock market
• Leveraged buy-out – financing or refinancing the assets of the business to generate the cash to purchase the equity stake held by the financial backer.

Team effort. Although this is a team effort, and you may well have equal shareholdings or be risking equal amounts of money, one person has to take the leadership role. It is vitally important to ensure that everyone understands and accepts what roles each member of the team is going to play after the buy-out.

When you have done the deal you have a business to run. It's important that you step up and take the tough decisions when necessary. You may find that some members of the team are just not up to the leadership role – and you will have divided loyalties. They helped you complete the MBO, they are friends and shareholders with you, but your duty and responsibilities are to all the shareholders.

It is for this reason that you must have a shareholders agreement. This vital document will set out what happens when someone leaves (for cause or by choice) or is ill. It will set out a method for valuing the shares in the event of a departure, and a way of resolving disputes (perhaps through third party arbitration). It may also set out matters that must be agreed by a majority of shareholders.

If you delay the tough decisions, you are just storing up trouble for yourself. Problems are best dealt with when they are still small problems.

The Corporate Seller
Many of the same restrictions and challenges apply to the situation where the vendor is a larger business, but there are some key differences.

Carving out.
It's quite likely that the business you are buying is a business unit, not a stand-alone business, and one challenge is that the business relies upon services and support from other parts of the corporate entity. That can be as simple as a group insurance policy, but might well be reliance upon a shared service centre where all the "back-office" functions take place.

If you are competing to buy the business with external buyers, there's a good chance you can claim an advantage here. For the vendor to setup replacement systems and complete the "carve out" of the business to be sold is both time consuming and expensive. You can agree a fee for the vendor to continue to support you for a few months whilst you get setup – and take away all the pain.

Speed
Once the group has made the decision to sell, they typically want to get a deal done just as soon as possible so that they can focus on the core business. A trade sale to an external buyer will usually take several months to complete. You can move much faster – you already know the business so your due diligence will be much quicker. In a trade sale, the vendor or their

agent has to approach the potential buyers and ascertain their interest then the buyer has to study the business.

Case Study: This is a recent press release describing a fairly typical MBO of a division that is no longer core to the parent company. It's also worth noting that the parent, Greencore plc has been under some financial stress recently.

Ministry of Cake acquired in MBO

A four-strong senior management team has completed a buyout of a Taunton-based dessert manufacturer.

Ministry of Cake supplies popular cakes and desserts that appear on the menus of pubs and restaurants across the UK. Chief executive Chris Ormrod led the MBO team along with finance director Jeremy French, operations director John Anderson and sales director Steve Braithwaite.

The Taunton business employs around 250 people and has an annual turnover of £25 million. The company is the UK's leading producer of chocolate fudge cake but also has a broad range of other sweets. Formed in 1865 by renowned sweet entrepreneur William Tanner Maynard, the firm has reportedly experienced significant growth in recent years.

The previous owner, listed food producer Greencore plc, put Ministry of Cake up for sale four months ago and the internal buyout is thought to have been for an upfront cash consideration of £8 million and a deferred consideration of up to £3 million. The private equity provider LDC, which is part of the Lloyds Banking Group, backed the MBO.

The company produces more than two million slices of cake every week, with its clients including Pizza Hut, Hard Rock Café and Café Nero, as well as a number of pub chains.

Chris Ormrod said: "LDC's investment brings additional strategic input and financial backing to our business and will help us to deliver ambitious growth plans. (Pollard, 2014)

Legacy Shareholding

It is also possible that the corporate vendor will be prepared to hold a stake in the business that you can buy over a number of years – effectively vendor financing – but if the corporate is in good financial standing the pressure to complete the disposal may be less.

Vendor Loans

In a similar fashion, the vendor in a corporate disposal may be prepared to lend money to the acquirers. They may well find better rates of return and they will of course regard the loans as being lower risk – they know the recipients of the loans.

A distressed seller

Sometimes, the owner of the business – be that a corporate or a private owner – will be distressed seller. There is some personal or financial pressure driving the need to dispose of the business.

As a buyer in the MBO space, their reason for sale is unimportant but the distress always means they want a quick deal, and you can move very quickly. You may find that you can get a bargain.

6 SUCCESSFULLY BUYING A BUSINESS

Buying a business is really easy. Just put enough money on the table, and the lucky vendor will happily sell to you. Buying a business and making a success of the deal, and more importantly the combined business after you have done the deal, is considerably harder.

Most acquisitions fail to meet or exceed expectations, and the business news is littered with stories and examples of deals gone wrong, from one of the largest corporate write-offs in history (AOL & Time Warner) through to the more recent RBS acquisition of ABN Amro at the top of the market.

Despite the press, most successful companies have used acquisitions as a part of their growth strategy, and for some it is the main driver of their growth.

"Done well, acquisitions can boost growth and provide an almost unmatched capability for rapid market entry; done badly, financial value, staff morale, and customer focus all can quickly drain away and take years to recover." (Vernerey)

Why <u>you</u> should consider acquisitions.

There no such thing as a stand-alone acquisitions strategy. Acquisitions can be used as part of an overall strategy to do many things:

- Solve a problem
- Kick start growth
- Diversify
- Enter new markets
- Develop new products
- And many more......

The key is that acquisition should be part of a strategy, and that acquisition planning must weigh the risks and potential rewards, just as in any other investment strategy.

"strategic rationale for an acquisition that creates value typically conforms to at least one of the following five archetypes: improving the performance of the target company, removing excess capacity from an industry, creating market access for products, acquiring skills or technologies more quickly or at lower cost than they could be built in-house, and picking winners early and helping them develop their businesses." (Marc Goedhart, 2010)

Many acquisition in the Small and Medium sized enterprise (SME) marketplace are poorly planned and executed. A typical deal in the sector is the purchase of a distressed business at an apparent bargain price, or the purchase of a business where the vendor is a long standing business acquaintance or friend of the purchaser. Such a deal may work out, but in my experience that is rare. It's difficult to measure results when there wasn't a target or a plan for the combined business.

Strategy and Risk

Understanding the risk attached to the acquisition strategy that you are considering will be crucial to your success.

One way of looking at risk is to use the Ansoff matrix:

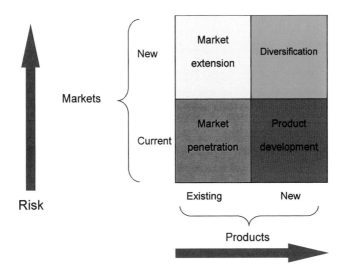

Examples may make this easier to understand.

In the UK, a number of household names have successfully used acquisitions as part of their strategy.

Tesco acquired T&S Stores – a chain of convenience stores - as a means of entering a new market sector – which in Ansoff terms would be a **Market Extension.**

The acquisition of T&S Stores enabled Tesco to start operating 800 convenience stores the day after the acquisition. Consider the alternative of organic growth, and the amount of time, effort and resource required achieving similar foothold and you can see how acquisitions can provide a shortcut to success.

Market Penetration

In the same sector as Tesco, Morrison's acquisition of Safeway represents Market Penetration. Although this is intrinsically lower risk, it has taken several years for this acquisition to bear fruit, at least partly because the Morrison's management team underestimated the resources required to integrate the two businesses.

Product Development through acquisition

Acquisitions can provide a step change in a business that is not possible, in the same time-frame, through organic growth. An obvious example of this is the purchase of a business that owns a product that has taken years to develop. You might well be able to create that same product in-house, but it will take time. If you buy the business you can dramatically reduce product development time.

This is very common in the IT Industry and one illustration is Sage Software's offering of accounting and ERP systems. Sage began as a provider of accounting systems for the smaller businesses, but through acquisition can now offer systems for businesses of many different types and sizes.

Diversification is the strategy with the highest risk

This was very common in the 1970's and 1980's. You may remember Hanson Group, Williams Holdings and others acquiring substantial, unrelated businesses. More recently, diversifiers have looked for some commonality of customer, product or service, positioning the strategy close to the very centre of the matrix.

There can be many other reasons to consider acquisitions

Capacity driven

Every successful growing business will suffer from capacity constraints during the life cycle. Growth is never a straight line, but looked at in fine detail a series of steps as capacity is adjusted to cope with new levels of business. Buying a business to obtain its capacities, whether that is plant and machinery or human, is a way to smooth the steps and perhaps move up several steps at one time.

Resolving business weaknesses.

Over time, even the best managed business can start to develop weaknesses. Perhaps a supplier has become vital to the business, but is proving unreliable. Bringing that product or service in-house is one way to eliminate that weakness.

Warning: this is dangerous territory.

Studies have shown that most acquisitions fail to deliver value for shareholders.

One study evaluated the stock market reaction to 600 acquisitions over a period between 1975 and 1991. Acquiring firms suffered an average 4 per cent drop in market value (after adjusting for market movements) in the three months following the acquisition announcement. Finally, a 1994 study conducted jointly by Business Week and Mercer Management Consulting, Inc. analysed 150 acquisitions (worth more than $500 million) from July 1990 to July 1995. Based on total stock returns from three months before the announcement and up to three years after the announcement:

30 per cent substantially eroded shareholder returns.
20 per cent eroded some returns.
33 per cent created only marginal returns.
17 per cent created substantial returns.

Assuming that no CEO would ever announce the goal of only breaking even, these results suggest that less than one in five acquisitions lives up to its initial expectations. If future results were reasonably predictable, most acquisitions simply would not occur.

Harvard's Michael Porter (1987) notes "There's a tremendous allure to mergers and acquisitions. It's the big play, the dramatic gesture. With one stroke of the pen you can add billions to size, get a front-page story, and create excitement in markets."

The rewards can be great

Bain reports

You ignore deal making at your peril. Companies that did no acquisitions between 2000 and 2010 turned in poorer performance than the deal makers. The more deals a company did, and the more material those deals were, the better its performance was likely to be (Marc Goedhart, 2010)

Cisco use acquisitions as a core part of their strategy
Cisco's growth strategy is based on identifying and driving market transitions. Corporate Development focuses on acquisitions that help Cisco capture these market transitions.

Cisco segments acquisitions into three categories: market acceleration, market expansion, and new market entry. The target companies might bring different types of assets to Cisco, including great talent and technology, mature products and solutions, or new go-to-market and business models. Cisco particularly seeks acquisitions with the potential to reach billion dollar markets.

Integration is essential to successful acquisitions. Our overall business development effort includes engaging from the early diligence phase through to mainstream business, by investing in dedicated integration resources across the company at the corporate and functional levels. We have a long history of integration, achieving best practices through continuous learning and deep experience with a process that challenges all companies who repeatedly make acquisitions. (Cisco)

Before you start – two key questions:

Acquisitions can transform a business, but they are not to be undertaken lightly. They require a considerable commitment of management time and expertise.

Do you have the resources to make this happen?

They are not a "quick fix" and should not be part of your strategy if you cannot commit to following through.

Do you, as the business leader, have the time?

If you are working 6 days a week, acquisitions are not something to consider. Perhaps start by engaging additional support so that you have the time. Professional advisors will help with the entire acquisition process, but they will need your input and the combined business will need your leadership.

Making Successful Acquisitions

Your first step on the road to successful acquisitions is to determine and test your strategy. The stronger the strategy, the better will be your chances of success. Test your strategy through discussion with your advisors (not just the corporate finance advisor) and if you have the opportunity with your peers. Time spent on the strategy is always time well spent.

From the strategy you can start to develop acquisition criteria and an acquisition brief. A tightly drawn brief will save you time and money and help your advisors be more successful in finding suitable businesses.

Acquisitions are a project, and a fundamental foundation for any successful project is the well-defined brief.

Bain, the consulting group, use this model:

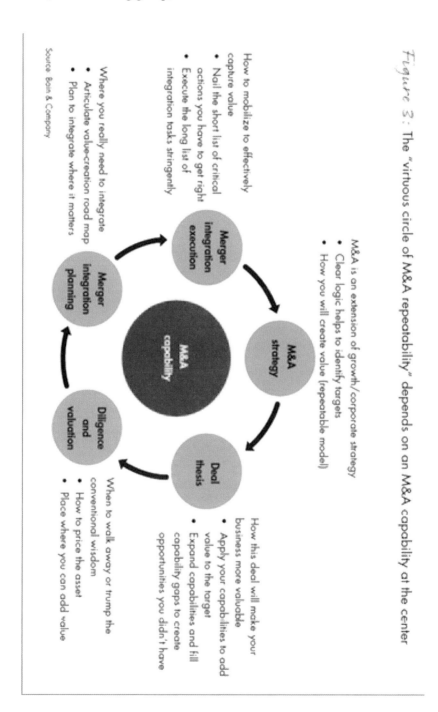

Figure 3: The "virtuous circle of M&A repeatability" depends on an M&A capability at the center

- M&A is an extension of growth/corporate strategy
- Clear logic helps to identify targets
- How you will create value (repeatable model)

How this deal will make your business more valuable
- Apply your capabilities to add value to the target
- Expand capabilities and fill capability gaps to create opportunities you didn't have

When to walk away or trump the conventional wisdom
- How to price the asset
- Place where you can add value

Where you really need to integrate
- Articulate value-creation road map
- Plan to integrate where it matters

How to mobilize to effectively capture value
- Nail the short list of critical actions you have to get right
- Execute the long list of integration tasks stringently

Source: Bain & Company

Circle labels: Merger integration execution; M&A strategy; Deal thesis; Diligence and valuation; Merger integration planning; M&A capability (center)

The strategy will drive the formation of the acquisition criteria ("Deal Thesis" in Bain's model); the more tightly the criteria are drawn, the more likely you are to achieve a result in line with your strategy.

There are many characteristics of the target business that you will need to consider, some of which will be more important to your strategy than others.

It's a good idea to start with the ideal business, then work back from there to categorize the features that are "Must have" and the features that are "would be nice" and of course there will probably be a "must not have" set of attributes.

Broadly, you can break the characteristics into major groups. I use these:

- What does the business do?
    - Is this business doing what we do or something else?
- Who does it do it for?
    - What kind of customers / markets?
- How does it do it?
    - Do they use a similar business model to our own?
- What intangible assets does it possess?
    - Are we buying the IP?
- Who owns it now?
    - How complicated will it be?
- Geographic Base
    - Do we need it to be based near us, or can we manage a remote operation?
- Financial Characteristics
    - Only profitable & successful, or start-up, or turnaround & receivership options?
- What kind of deal are we / they looking for?
    - Do we want complete ownership? Or do we want the managers co-investing to keep them interested and focused.

One way to consider some of the questions posed in drawing up tight criteria and a good brief for your advisers is to use the mind map on the following pages.

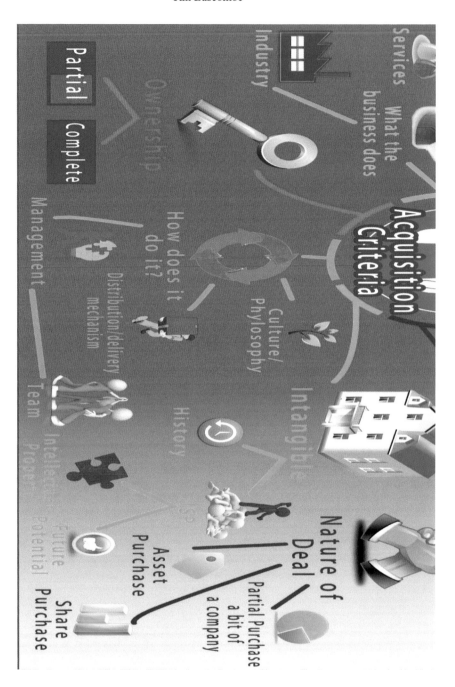

It may well be that you are unable to answer all the questions posed by the mind-map; answering the questions will help refine the strategy.

☐

8 steps to successful acquisitions.

Hopefully by now you will have realized that successful acquisitions require considerable resources, both financial and in management time.

Attempting to leap straight to the top step is likely to create a raft of problems.

This is teamwork.

Once you have drawn up your criteria, it is time to select the research, deal and integration teams.

Your research team should have knowledge of your target market and access to databases – typically proprietary information providers for that market / sector / geography.

Your deal team needs to include skills ranging from financial and negotiation to HR skills. You may also need technical skills (depending upon your industry) and/or operations skills and knowledge.

Your integration team will be crucial to your success. There may be some overlap with the deal and research teams, but it is important that the integration team members do not lead on the negotiations. This team needs to know your business inside and out and have excellent people management and communication skills.

The key individual in the research and deal teams will be your corporate finance adviser.

Choose someone you trust, and whose advice you will take. If you don't know someone, ask your other trusted advisors for recommendations.

Choose someone who deals with businesses like yours, of a similar size and in a similar sector.

If you are running an engineering business and your adviser usually works with small retail outlets, there will be a mismatch and at best a steep learning curve.

The adviser will work with the research team, guiding and directing their research to create the long-list, and will then represent your business in the stages that follow.

- They will deal with all confidentiality issues
- They will lead negotiations with the target
- They will help with raising funding (where required) to complete the transaction
- They will project manage the deal through due diligence and the legal process to completion
- They will keep you informed and aware of issues as they arise in the deal, and of issues to be dealt with post acquisition by the integration team.

Research

Once you have your teams in place you can commence the market research and analyse your chosen market place. This is a time consuming exercise, comparing search results to the criteria you have developed to reduce the number of candidate companies.

The first stage of this uses publicly available records and information, for example from credit reference agencies and market data providers.

Typically, well defined criteria will allow researchers to generate a long list of around 100 targets.

Refining this long list to a more manageable number is time intensive; individual company website reviews, analysis of published articles and comment in trade press and on social media are some of the tools. Corporate descriptions included in recruitment advertising are often a good source.

That more detailed analysis compares the targets to the criteria established. It is important to stick to the strategy and not to flex the "must-have" category at this point – if it doesn't match, discard it.

Approach

The refined list provides the basis for the next step, which is the first contact between the target company and your advisor.

The advisor will make a subtle approach to the majority owner (if there is one) or to the Chairman / MD of the target company. The purpose of the approach is to gather further information on the target, and to ascertain if there is any interest in a further discussion.

The approach must be subtle, even somewhat indirect. The owner may not be considering the sale of his business, and indeed may not ever have considered selling his business. The direct question "would you consider selling your business?" is likely to get more negative responses than "We'd like to talk to you about a closer working relationship, might you be interested?"

The objective of the approach is to get a face to face meeting.

The first meeting

If your target company was not on the open market, and your corporate finance advisor has had a positive response to the initial enquiry, it is time for you, as the principal, to get involved.

For the owner of the target business, especially if they were not planning to sell, this is a challenging meeting. They will have (at best) mixed emotions and many doubts and fears.

You job is to put them at ease and make friends; if you don't get on with them you almost certainly will not gather enough information to table an acceptable offer, and you probably need their co-operation to ensure a successful transfer of the business to your ownership.

Find occasion to praise the business they have built; you may be thinking otherwise, but this could well be their life's work and they will have pride.

Reassure the owner of you intentions (where you can) towards the business and the team; share the vision of your strategy for the combined business to enthuse them.

Information Exchange

You will want to learn as much as possible about the target company so that you can confirm it does indeed meet your requirements and match the criteria.

The vendor will want to know about your plans and ambitions; they will be very nervous about releasing information and it is often at this stage you will sign a confidentiality or non-disclosure agreement.

When you have confirmed, usually as a result of the first round of information provided by the target, that the business is a good match then it is time to gather sufficient information (mostly financial) to put a value on the business so that you can make an offer.

See the chapter on Valuation for guidance on how to value a business.

Negotiation

One of the keys to making a success of acquisitions is to negotiate the right deal. If the vending shareholders aren't required or will have no interest in the on-going business, then the deal can be one-sided in your favour, but most of the time you will want their help and assistance, at least for a while, after the deal completes. It makes sense to craft a win-win deal, and understand the vendor's priorities.

It also makes sense to minimise your potential losses.

It is quite unlikely that a deal will be all cash on completion – this is not like buying a house or a car. You will want some form of guarantee of future financial performance, and one way to do that is to tie part of the consideration to the continued efforts of the exiting owner.

You may also wish to minimise your cash outlay at completion; there may be challenges in obtaining finance, so perhaps loan notes and or/equity based compensation will also come into play.

What might be important to the vendor might be unimportant to you and vice-versa; this is really a situation where knowledge is power.

Sometimes it is a good idea to have someone negotiating who is not going to have operational responsibility for the business, after the acquisition. They may be heightened emotions and strong feelings during the negotiation, after all!

"We have a firm principle that the people who will be managing the company post-acquisition are not involved in the negotiations..." (Vernerey)

It is almost always a requirement to negotiate in a friendly manner; the vendors will not (usually) sell to someone they don't like – and they will find a reason to justify their decision.

There's really no substitute for experience in this area; any error in overpaying for a business, or agreeing the wrong terms, or falling out with the key employees is likely to cause many years of pain.

Presenting the proposed deal is the best possible light is important. Yes, you are negotiating to buy a business, but at the same time you are selling the idea of the deal – no one is forcing the vendor to sell to you.

Your negotiation strategy and style has to take account of these factors, but long before you enter the room you need to establish:

The ideal position. What is your aim, what are you going to ask for, what is the best you could possibly get?

The walk-away point. This is the position at which the deal is no longer worth doing, even though you may have invested considerable time and effort up to this point. If you don't have this firmly established, you risk getting "deal fever" and creating more problems later down the road.

Try looking at the situation from the other side of the table – indeed it can help to role play this, with someone taking the other side. Try to estimate their ideal position, and their walk-away point.

Use that understanding to build a list of give-aways. These are things that have little value to you, but are important for the other side. You will use some of them in the negotiation, trading a give-away in return for something you want.

Integration

Many examples of acquisitions that fail to meet expectations can be directly traced to poor integration programmes, and failures either in strategy or in execution.

In the UK, one excellent example of integration failure was the acquisition by Morrison's supermarkets of the Safeway chain. Strategically, it was undoubtedly the right move, but the post-acquisition effort was lamentable. No one doubted the abilities of the Morrison's team to run the stores – in fact they were amongst the best performers in the sector – but integrating an acquisition, especially a substantial one, requires a dedicated experienced team. It is interesting to note that the eventual success of Morrison's Safeway came about under a new management team.

There are many degrees of integration, from total absorption right through to leaving the acquired business operating as a stand-alone unit. What is important is to have a plan and an execution process, which will include a substantial communications effort.

Acquired businesses can be integrated at many different degrees, ranging from total absorption right through to "stand alone" where very few changes are made. There are no right and wrong methodologies.

Successful integration always starts with the planning phase and the plan is amended and updated as knowledge is acquired during the due diligence and discovery phases.

When the deal completes, speed is of the essence. I know of one acquirer, who, as we completed the acquisition, said to the vendor who had just handed over his business "thank goodness we managed to complete tonight. I'm flying off for my holiday tomorrow!"

How does that statement make the new team feel valued and important?

You need a plan for the first 100 minutes, 100 hours, and 100 days.

You need a strong integration team (this is where Morrison's failed) who will be not only in charge, but able to answer all the questions that will result from the acquisition.

Communication is vitally important. Individuals at all levels of the business will have doubts and questions, people are afraid of change and of the unknown.

"When Cingular Wireless and AT&T Wireless Services closed on their $41 billion merger in October 2004, the new entity hit the ground running. Training programs were launched, call centers were staffed with thousands of temporary customer service representatives to handle an anticipated spike in inquiries, and the two companies' IT systems were combined. And it all happened before the end of the first post-merger day of business" (Ravi Chanmugam, 2005)

"At Novel, a huge amount of our growth was through acquisitions, but the part of those deals that really mattered was the post-acquisition strategy to integrate the new entity. One thing that stood out about doing it right was to offer people in the acquired company preference in jobs within the company effectively moving them out of the acquired company while at the same time, encouraging people within the company to transfer into the newly acquired division." (Murray, 2014)

How not to do it
There are hundreds of examples of failed acquisitions and we can learn some lessons from them.

For many years, the most famous was AOL / Time Warner which led to (at the time) the largest write-off in corporate history.

Examining the transaction, it's difficult not to conclude that AOL was over-valued, but equally it was the clash of the very different cultures that stands out.

Other famous failures include BMW's purchase of Rover and the short lived Daimler Chrysler business. BMW not only took on a failing business, it did so without the management resources to drive through change and without an understanding of the strength of the British trade unions. They salvaged the Mini brand, but that was an expensive acquisition.

There was a rumour that in Daimler Chrysler's case, the management was divided between the US and Germany. Executives with a base in Germany and teams in the US (and vice-versa) found that their instructions were ignored or wilfully misinterpreted.

Success Stories

Successful acquisitions are much more rarely reported, but it is unusual in the extreme for a business to grow solely through organic means. Highly acquisitive companies abound in the technology and pharmaceutical sectors.

In grocery retail, consider Tesco's entry to the convenience store format through the purchase of T&S stores. Tesco gained 5% of the convenience store market with 850 stores; the organic route to the same goal would have taken many years, even with an aggressive store opening program.

Acquisitions don't have to be on a grand scale. The sweet spot, in terms of size, tends to be a ratio of somewhere between 3:1 and 10:1. If the business you are buying is more than 1/3 the size of your existing business, it may well be difficult to integrate and will consume significant management time. If it is less than one tenth of your existing business, it will not deliver major change. There are always exceptions, but the most notable is the acquisition of intellectual property, where the business being acquired can be relatively very small.

Conclusion

There's an old story about a journalist on a foreign assignment who wasn't filing any stories. When queried by his editor, he responded with the line "No news is good news" to be told that "No news means no job".

The stories you see in the news are those of the disastrous acquisitions where something went badly wrong or the target company was a "national treasure."

You don't see in the main news the hundreds of acquisitions that are completed every day, but if you look at any successful company acquisitions will play a part in their strategy for growth.

Business owners and managers who fail to consider acquisitions do harm to their businesses and their relative value. If you are not making acquisitions, perhaps your competitors are one step ahead of you.

Bibliography:

Cisco. (n.d.).

Marc Goedhart, T. K. (2010, July). The five types of successful acquisitions. *McKinsey & Copmany Insights*.

Murray, E. (2014). *LinkedIn*.

Ravi Chanmugam, W. S. (2005). The intelligent clean room: ensuring value. *VOL. 26 NO. 3 2005*.

Vernerey, L. -S. (n.d.). Acquisitions by degree. *CEOforum.com.au*.

Pollard, D. (2014). Business Sale Report. Business Sale.

Borzomato, M. (2014). *Insider north-west.* Insider Media.

ABOUT THE AUTHOR

In one of his first roles after achieving his accounting qualifications, Tim Luscombe was responsible for the financial management and reporting of a recently acquired business. That became a post-acquisition integration role and led to his joining the research and deal teams.

Later in his career, Tim was part of the team that took a UK company to IPO on NASDAQ and was subsequently based in Hong Kong for a number of years developing businesses across Asia Pacific.

Tim ran his own property business before returning to the corporate world to execute and integrate the acquisitions of several owner managed service businesses as leader of a US technology business.

Tim has been advising on strategy, finance, acquisitions and company sales since 2002. He leads a team of business advisors and is a partner in a corporate finance advisory firm.

You can find out more and get in touch at

www.dealfinancebook.com
www.timluscombe.co.uk

Made in the USA
Charleston, SC
24 July 2014